What Is
ATHEISM?

A

Short

Introduction

DOUGLAS
E. KRUEGER

 Prometheus Books

59 John Glenn Drive
Amherst, New York 14228-2197

Published 1998 by Prometheus Books

02 01 00 99 98   5 4 3 2 1

Library of Congress Cataloging-in-Publication Data

Krueger, Douglas E.
    What is atheism? : a short introduction / Nicholas E. Krueger.
        p.   cm.
    Includes bibliographical references.
    ISBN 1–57392–214–5 (pbk. : alk. paper)
    1. Atheism. I. Title.
BL2747.3.K735   1998
211'.8—dc21   98–16023
                                                         CIP

Printed in the United States of America on acid-free paper.

Acknowledgments

Many people have contributed to the creation of this book. Free-thinkers such as Thomas Paine, Voltaire, Robert Ingersoll, and Bertrand Russell have played a role through the inspiration of their works, which have provided both instruction and solace.

Of those more directly involved, many thanks go to Gregory Klebanoff, who was especially helpful with the books's preparation, as well as with issues involving Question #7. Question #4 benefitted greatly from the expertise of Darrel Henschell. Michael Martin's insightful comments regarding definitions and other important matters vastly improved the book. Ted Drange's contributions, especially the argument from nonbelief, were invaluable. The patience of my family while I worked here and there, early and late, was especially appreciated. Others, such as Bob McCoy, Dick Bennett, and assorted folk at the University of Arkansas, have helped tremendously with their encouragement.

Finally, I can never fully express my heartfelt gratitude for the support of Gretchen Pedersen. She deserves a great deal of credit for showing me the value of including Question #8, offering a pro-fuse flow of encouragement, and assisting in many other important concerns, both literary and otherwise, for which I will forever be in her debt.

Contents

Preface

"Mr. Krueger, do you believe in the wind?"

I could hardly believe it. Here, at an institution for higher learning, I was being asked this question!

"I mean, you can't see it," she continued. "So if you don't believe in god, how can you believe in the wind?" She finished her question and awaited her answer. Whether she really thought she'd stumped me with it, or whether she was simply confused about my position and wanted clarification, I don't know. Whatever the motive, it was clear that she asked the question seriously. It was also clear that she was not the only student present who thought that this was a good question.

I gave my answer, but I was rather piqued. I was standing at a lecture podium in front of over three hundred people who had gathered to watch a debate between an atheist and a theist. I was the atheist, and I had spent quite a bit of time earlier in the evening carefully explaining how we can rationally conclude that there is no god without first being omniscient. Just a few minutes earlier, in

9

fact, I had answered two other questions about how we can conclude that there is no god. None of these reasons had *anything* to do with invisibility. So why was someone asking about the wind?

Looking back on it now, it is easy to laugh about such a ridiculous question. However, it is also easy to feel disheartened. These were, after all, *college* students at this debate! They are supposed to be some of the most intelligent members of the community, yet many of them betrayed a profound ignorance of the issues related to their belief in god. Atheism is an important and intellectually powerful alternative to the religious outlook so prevalent today, yet it is one of the most misunderstood philosophical positions in our society. Most people have no idea what atheism is. All too often, religious leaders will spread misinformation in an effort to keep their flock in line by threats and falsehoods. In some cases they have even told their followers that atheists worship the devil, or that there aren't really any atheists at all!

The religious point of view is so deeply embedded into our culture, and it becomes a basic part of the worldview of theists so early in life, that it is no small task to challenge such a firmly rooted set of beliefs, beliefs which many people cherish as dearly as life itself. It is also no accident that belief in gods holds such a place in people's lives. Throughout human history religious leaders have used various means of argumentation, coercion, and deception to ensure that their followers are unaware or greatly misinformed about alternative ways of thinking. They have had much success. In his *History of My Religious Opinions from 1833 to 1839,* for example, the influential British churchman Cardinal Newman (1801–1890) stated:

> It would be a gain to the country were it vastly more superstitious, more bigoted, more gloomy, more fierce in its religion than at present it shows itself to be. . . . From the age of fifteen,

dogma has been the fundamental principle of my religion: I know of no other religion; I cannot enter into the idea of any other sort of religion. . . .[1]

Can the development of bigotry and narrow-mindedness be a virtue? Even today there are a number of religious denominations which forbid their members, under threat of expulsion, to read *or even own* any material which expresses dissent. Is it any wonder that so many people are so uninformed about atheism?

Part of the problem, too, is that it is difficult to find introductory works about atheism. Although some philosophers have published excellent, lengthy, detailed defenses of atheism—and of course there is a place for extended argument and precision—those most in need of this information about atheism, those without formal philosophical training, would find such complex works too frustrating. Some religious writers hostile to atheism have published accessible books which claim to both explain and refute atheism, but these works usually distort the atheist view and thus fall far short of refuting it. In the end, people curious about atheism are left to the mercy of those unscrupulous persons who believe that it is to their advantage to keep people as ignorant as possible on this subject. There is a need for a concise introduction to atheism which avoids the technical analysis of the professional philosopher yet which sacrifices little accuracy. This book has been written in the hope that it will help fill this void.

This book answers eight questions which are both important for an understanding of atheism and representative of the type of questions which are often asked of atheists. The different subheadings of the responses are indicated by a capital letter, and divisions within each of those sections are demarcated by an arabic numeral and subheading, a lower-case letter and a subheading, a parenthetical lower-case roman numeral, a parenthetical capital letter, and so on, in descending order of scope. I hope that this system makes it easier, not harder, for the reader to locate material and follow the flow of the argument than it would have been otherwise. I sometimes include a summary of each major section before proceeding to the next section or chapter. Many of these theistic arguments, as well as my own atheistic ones, have been put in premise/conclusion format, and, for clarity, I have left some of the more obvious premises implied. The fact that the general populace is so ignorant of views other than that of theism ensures that there will be many other questions about atheism which space does not permit to be included in this work. A list of suggested readings and other resources has been included as a guide to further answers.

In our culture Christianity is the most widespread religion which asserts the existence of god, so Christianity will often be used throughout this work as representative of the theistic view. Christians are my target audience, so much of what is said by way of critique will be directed toward that view instead of, say, the religions of the Norse gods, the Greek gods, or others. However, most of what can be said of Christianity may also be said of other versions of theism, their claims about their gods, and their holy books.

I harbor no illusions about the possibility of changing the minds of theists. Most have believed in god since childhood and will never abandon that belief. These people have never been taught how to think clearly and carefully about religious matters, and they will strongly resist doing so for the remainder of their lives. However, it is my hope that this work may free some theists from the intellectual domination born of fear and ignorance and allow those thoughtful men and women to make an informed choice about how they should view their lives and the universe in which they live. If this book can do this for even a few readers, then perhaps I am not just whistling in the wind.

Note

1. *Oxford Dictionary of Quotations*, 3d ed. (New York: Oxford University Press, 1980), p. 361.

Question #1

What Is Atheism?

A. Atheism may be defined as the view that there are no gods.

There are two views which are often considered atheism—the broad version (that of not assenting to the theistic view) and the narrow version (the claim that the theistic view is false). Each is defined by the manner in which it denies the claims of theism, so we would do well to first consider the theistic claim before defining atheism.

1. Theism will be defined as the view that the traditional god exists.

Theism is often broadly defined as the view that there is *at least* one god. Monotheists hold that there is exactly one god, while

15

polytheists claim that there are more than one. However, most the-ists in our culture are monotheists who assert that there is exactly one god, no more and no less. They further claim that this god has the traditional attributes of being omnipotent (all-powerful), omni-scient (all-knowing), omnibenevolent (all-good), and transcendent (outside of space and time). These theists also claim that this god takes an active interest in human events, as opposed to, say, the god of deists, who has all the attributes of the god of the theists, but who is not involved in human affairs at all. Deists usually hold that the only evidence for the existence of god is the existence of the universe and its design, and perhaps the existence of moral values, yet they insist that these factors do not admit of any but the most general claims about the nature of god. For the deist, this evi-dence does not lead to any specific claims about the intentions or identity of the supreme being, certainly not that god intervenes in human affairs with miracles or with explicit commands regarding conduct. Knowledge of god through revelation is rejected by the deist. Many of the founding fathers, including Thomas Jefferson, were deists, incidentally.

Because of its popularity, the view which will be most at issue in this work is the popular monotheistic view in which god is said to have the traditional attributes and is also supposedly concerned with human activity. This is a conception of god shared by Christians, Jews, Muslims, and other monotheists. Throughout this work I will refer to this kind of monotheism as "theism," although much of the criticism will also apply to polytheism, deism, and other kinds of belief in gods.

2. *There are two definitions of atheism.*

The term "atheism" is from the Greek *atheos*. The prefix "a" means "without," and the Greek *theos* means "god," so atheism means simply "being without god." Theism asserts that there is a god, so atheism is the view which does not assert that there is a god. However, there are two ways to refrain from asserting that there is a god.

a. *The atheist does not assert that there are gods.*

On the broad definition, an atheist is simply one who does not agree with the theist that there is a god. This broad definition of atheism has been historically more prevalent. Until the term "agnosticism" became popular, there was no clear distinction between agnosticism and what we now call atheism.

"Agnosticism" is a term coined by Thomas Huxley in 1869.[1] He meant it to refer to someone who suspends judgment on the matter of god's existence and other supernatural claims. Some agnostics believe that there is not enough evidence about whether or not god exists to reach a definitive judgment on the issue. They hold that until such facts are gathered, lest one commit the fallacy of an appeal to ignorance, one should not affirm or deny the existence of such beings. In logic, an appeal to ignorance—called *argumentum ad ignoratiam* in Latin—is a well-known fallacy in reasoning in which one concludes from the fact that something has not been proven to be true or proven to be false with certainty that it is, in fact, say, true. For example: "No one has ever been able to prove whether or not George Washington ever slept in this bed. Therefore, I can conclude that he did." Obviously, the conclusion is unjustified given the lack of evidence. One class of agnostics insists that no one can show that god does or does not exist, so any attempt to claim that there is or is not a god will commit this logical fallacy. Note that in my response to Question #7, I argue that the claim that a god does not exist falls within an accepted category of exceptions to this logical principle. Other agnostics believe that it is impossible for the human mind to make a judgment about god's existence because the nature of the claim involves elements beyond the possibility of human experience. They believe that there will never be enough facts to decide the issue because the relevant information is beyond our ability to sense or comprehend. Regardless of the reason, each type of agnostic would refrain from agreeing with the theist, so on this broad definition it would follow that an agnostic would be considered an atheist.

b. The atheist denies that there are gods.

The narrow, stronger definition of "atheism" is that of someone who asserts that there are no gods. On this definition, an agnostic would not be considered an atheist. Although the broad use of the term "atheism" has its advantages, since it is much easier to defend, it will not be used here. I will confine my use of the term "atheism" to the stronger thesis that there are no gods. Although it is a stronger claim, it is defensible, and, in addition, it is the view to which I adhere. I agree with the agnostic that the theist's claim that there is a god is unwarranted, but I also believe that there are good reasons to think that the claim that there are no gods *is* warranted.

The following definitions, then, will be used:

Theism—the belief that there exists exactly one god, and this god is omnipotent, omniscient, omnibenevolent, and transcendent. This god is also active in the world.

The traditional god—the god of theism.

Deism—the belief that there exists exactly one god, and this god is omnipotent, omniscient, omnibenevolent, and transcendent. This god is *not* active in the world.

Polytheism—the belief that at least two gods exist, none of which is the god of theism.

Atheism—the belief that there are no gods.

B. There are many common misconceptions about atheism.

Many people are terribly misinformed about atheism. Some mistakenly believe one or more of the following with regard to atheism.

1. People become atheists so that they can do whatever they want.

It is a common mistake to think that atheists are those who want to abandon morality. People should adopt beliefs because they are true or likely to be true, and they should abandon beliefs because they have been discovered false, or likely to be false. The motive for belief should be truth, not some perceived reward. It does not follow from the fact that there is no god that everything is permitted. In fact, many atheists follow very strict moral codes of conduct. It is not part of the definition of an atheist that one abandons morality.

2. An atheist is one who hates god.

Atheists do not hate god. They cannot hate something which does not exist. Atheists are not rebelling against god. Someone who thinks that an atheist hates god just doesn't understand the definition of atheism.

3. An atheist is one who worships Satan.

Atheists don't believe that Satan or any other demon or deity exists, so they don't worship Satan or anyone else. Atheists do not believe in the existence of any supernatural beings. Those who think that atheists worship demons do not understand atheism.

4. Everyone worships something. An atheist must have some god.

Sometimes theists recognize that their beliefs are irrational, and, rather than try to defend the view, or justify it, they try to look for "partners in guilt." That is, in an attempt to show that they are not doing anything more outlandish than everyone else, theists sometimes state that everyone worships something, so they claim that they are just doing what everyone else does. They don't want to admit that someone without gods can get along in life just as well, or better, than one who needs to cling to belief in a god, so they simply assert, without evidence, that everyone has gods. This claim is false. Atheists do not worship anyone or anything.

To counter this, Christians sometimes define worship as "thinking that something is important in your life" or god is defined as "ultimate concern" or other broad notions. Such word play is pointless. These definitions are so vague that they would prove nothing religious about atheists, certainly not that they "worship" anything in any important sense. Atheists consider people and ideas important in their lives, but to call this "worship" is absurd. Believing that someone is important does not make that person a god. Atheists do not revere anything or anyone in the way that theists revere their god.

Atheists hold that certain things other than gods are important in their lives, not because they think that these things are more important than gods, but because they believe that *there are no gods.* Those who try to paint atheists as theists are tacitly admitting that they cannot confront the issue of atheism. They instead try to show that there aren't any atheists, but this is just a stubborn refusal to face the facts. There are atheists.

5. A person becomes an atheist because of a fight with the priest, pastor, reverend, etc.

Did you stop believing in the tooth fairy because you had a fight with your dentist? Perhaps some atheists start on the road to truth because of a disagreement with a particular person, but the motive for belief should be truth. In discussing atheism, the issue is whether it is true that there are no gods, not what led to the investigation into whether there are gods.

6. All atheists believe the same thing— view "x."

Many religious writers claim that some other view is an essential part of atheism, and they proceed to attack that other view in an attempt to counter atheism. The other view may be communism, egoism (selfishness), pessimism, existentialism, Darwinism, Freudianism, anarchism, etc. The misconception here is that atheism is a particular view of life or some aspect of life instead of the view that there are no gods. In *Atheism: The Case against God*, George H. Smith writes:

> Just as the failure to believe in magic elves does not entail a
> code of living or a set of principles, so the failure to believe in a
> god does not imply any specific philosophical system.[2]

Further, the label "atheist," writes Smith, "does *not* announce one's agreement with, or approval of, other atheists."[3] For example, I don't believe that there are magic elves, and, I suppose, neither does Reverend Billy Graham. However, this does not entail that Graham and I share any particular set of beliefs. Similarly, if I were to find out that a neighbor of mine is also an atheist, I could not conclude from that alone that we share any particular set of beliefs.

The claim that all atheists have the same set of beliefs is the cornerstone of many misguided and misleading Christian works which purport to refute atheism. It is quite common for Christian writers to declare that a particular person is a spokesperson for atheism and then proceed to criticize that person. Sometimes it is Friedrich Nietzsche, Karl Marx, Jean-Paul Sartre, or others. Some Christians are so misguided they even attack the *Christian* philosopher Kierkegaard!

These theists hope to refute atheism by attacking a particular atheist's philosophy. Such attempts are a waste of time. They are based on fallacious reasoning. Atheism is not the result of the view of a particular individual. There were atheists in ancient Greece, in the Middle Ages, in the nineteenth century, and there are atheists now. One could examine the views of an atheist from each of those points in history and find out why he or she was an atheist, and it is possible that each had a worldview unlike any of the others and reasons for being an atheist unlike the reasons of any of the others. There were atheists before communism, before the theory of evolution, before modern science, before psychoanalysis. Someone can be an atheist without believing any of those things. Indeed, there may be any number of other reasons why one might conclude that there are no gods, but, regardless of the reasons, if the conclusion is that there are no gods, then it is an atheistic view.

Atheism itself is not a worldview, it is not a philosophy of life. It is an important *part* of a larger view, but atheism alone is not supposed to be a comprehensive philosophy of life. Consider this example. You believe that there are no unicorns. Would it be reasonable to expect you to have a comprehensive philosophy of life based solely on that belief? Of course not. Similarly, the atheist believes that there are no gods. This is not, in itself, a worldview. It is not supposed to be. Atheism may be the *result* of a worldview, but it is not a comprehensive worldview itself. Thus, attempts to refute atheism by attacking a much larger philosophy, one which has atheism as one of its many parts, are fruitless. Theists who attack such positions mislead their followers into believing that atheism is some view other than what it truly is.

Atheism is the belief that there are no gods. It's that simple.

Notes

1. Thomas H. Huxley, "Agnosticism," reprinted in *An Anthology of Atheism and Rationalism*, Gordon Stein, ed. (Amherst, N.Y.: Prometheus Books, 1980), pp. 42–45. This anthology will be called "Stein" hereinafter.

2. George H. Smith, *Atheism: The Case against God* (Amherst, N.Y.: Prometheus Books, 1989), p. 21.

3. Ibid., p. 22.

Question # 2

How Can Atheists Have Morals?

The view that atheists cannot act according to a legitimate system of ethics is, while erroneous, quite common. Most theists hold that only the religious view can provide a foundation for morality. There are good reasons to suppose that this assertion is false. If it is false, then the burden on the atheist is lessened: if it turns out that atheists could not have morals, the theist could not fault atheists for not having an adequate moral theory if the theist does not have one either.

Further, if it can be shown that the theist does not have an adequate foundation for ethics and that the atheist *does have such a foundation*, then the atheist would not only have shown that the charge that atheists cannot have an adequate system of morality is groundless, but would have shown that atheism is preferable to the theistic view for those who think that morality is important. This will be my strategy, then. First I will show that there are good reasons to think that theism, specifically Christianity, is an inadequate foundation for morality, and, then I will show that there are powerful systems of ethics which do not in any way require belief in a god.

25

A. Theism is an inadequate foundation for morality.

Can it be shown, first of all, that theism cannot provide an adequate basis for morality? It can. I will attack both the theoretical and the practical sides of theistic morality. I will present a well-known objection to the view that god is the source of morality, and then I will show that the Christian bible is also an inadequate basis for morality.[1] That will be followed by a few common objections which a theist might raise and some responses to these objections.

1. The Euthyphro Dilemma is effective against the view that god is the source of morality.

The Euthyphro dilemma, named after some insightful points taken from Plato's dialogue *Euthyphro*, shows the failing of the divine command theory of ethics, which is the view that god is the source of morality. In the dialogue, the character Socrates, speaking for Plato, meets the character Euthyphro, who is on his way to court to prosecute his own father for the murder of a field laborer. For the Greeks, loyalty to one's relatives was a matter of great importance, so Socrates asks Euthyphro whether he is certain that this act will not be offensive to the gods; i.e., whether it is immoral. Euthyphro assures Socrates that he is an expert in matters pertaining to the wishes of the gods, and in the course of the discussion Euthyphro attempts to defend the divine command theory of ethics.[2] According-ing to this view, we know what is good only because god tells us what is good. However, as Plato asked over 2,000 years ago, does god command what is good because god recognizes what is good, or is it good *because* god commands it? That is the dilemma, and each of the options turns out to be undesirable to the theist.

a. One horn of the dilemma is that what is good is defined by the fact that it is god's will.

On the one hand, if something god commands is to be defined as good on the grounds that it is god's will, then the divine command theorist must admit that anything can be considered good as long as god commands it. It would make no sense to ask whether god's commands are good. God could command someone to bash infants to death, to commit genocide, to stone people to death (and other atrocities such as we find in the bible), and such things would *by definition* be good acts, since god has commanded them.

Would a Christian want to commit to such a system of ethics where *anything* goes? The philosopher Bertrand Russell notes:

> If the *only* basis of morality is God's decrees, it follows that they might just as well have been the opposite of what they are; no reason except caprice could have prevented the omission of all the "nots" from the Decalogue.[3]

In other words, the ten commandments (the Decalogue) could have been just the opposite of what they are and they would, on this view, still be good because they would still be the will of god and that is the definition of good. Theists who take this horn of the Euthyphro dilemma must admit that they really don't have a standard of ethics. What they have is a standard of obedience—they will do whatever god commands. Slavery, however, is not ethics.

It would also make no sense to say that god is good if god is the standard of goodness. After all, if god *is* good, in the sense that god

27

is identical with the standard of goodness, then to say "God is good" is merely to say "God is god," which is an uninformative statement. A devil worshiper could say the same thing about the being he or she worships—"Satan is what he is." The subject and the predicate are the same object, so the sentence is uninformative. The relationship between goodness and god loses its meaning if god is the standard of goodness, so "god is good" would say nothing.

Further, if one would like to know whether a given being is god, there would be no set of standards with which one could compare that being in order to identify it as god. For example, if one wants to know how to recognize a generous person, one could have a list of actions which one might expect a generous person to perform. The list could include such things as giving a certain percentage of one's income to the poor, handing out money when approached by beggars, volunteering at the local food bank, and other such activities. Similarly, the list could exclude activities such as obsessively hoarding money, refusing to share any part of an inheritance with one's siblings, and so on. The list of criteria is compiled using the concept of generosity. If the person measures up to the standard, then we can declare that person generous. In the case of god, however, there can be no such moral standard for theists who insist that god *is* the standard. There can be no list of criteria to identify whether a being is the good god. If god can perform or command *any* act because he sets the standard, what kinds of acts could possibly be put on an identification list? One could never say, "An evil being might command this, but god never would." No action could be required or ruled out with regard to god since that being could always decide to perform or command the opposite of any given criterion. After all, god sets the standard, doesn't he? Without an independent standard of moral or immoral acts against which to measure god, god could never be identified by his moral standing. Thus, morally speaking, there would be no way to distinguish being a slave to an evil demon as opposed to being a slave to god. In both cases the one doing the commanding could command anything whatsoever and carrying out that command would be, by definition, a good act. No act would be considered immoral in and of itself, or good in and of itself, apart from the issue of whether it has been commanded or forbidden. Anything from rape to murder would be considered good if it were commanded by the being who serves as the standard.

No act could be taboo for the being giving commands because that being who defines goodness would not have any independent standard of morality by which it could be limited to a certain set of acts. The being could not be bound by any moral code.

The only immoral act, on this view, is disobedience. The follower would be committed to a system of blind obedience to a being who cannot be meaningfully called good. Clearly, this option is undesirable for the theist.

b. The other horn of the dilemma is that god recognizes what is good and then wills what is good.

On the other hand, if the theist chooses the other horn of the dilemma, that god commands that which god recognizes as good, then the theist is admitting that there is a standard of goodness independent of god, and is, in fact, admitting that god is *not* the source of morality. In other words, if the view is that god in some way "sees" what is good and then tells us what to do on the basis of that, then god is not the source of morality, since the act god commands was *observed* to be good by god, not *made* good by god. God becomes, at best, merely an intermediary or a reporter about ethics, but he is not its source. This option, too, is undesirable for the theist, since it admits that god is not the source of ethics, and if god is not the source of ethics then there is nothing in principle which could show that the atheist cannot have an ethical system also.

Thus, the theist must choose between admitting that he or she has no standard of ethics but merely a principle of slavery, or admitting that god is not the source of morality. Neither option allows for the possibility that god is the source of a system of ethics. The Euthyphro dilemma has been conclusive in showing that the divine command theory of ethics *cannot* work, and no theist has ever been able to overcome this strong objection to the view that god is the source of ethics.

2. The bible is also an inadequate source for moral principles.

The first critique of theistic ethics was theoretical. This second part addresses the source which many Christians claim shows them, in practice, what god's will is—the bible.

a. It is not clear that many principles in the bible are intended to be ethical.

In the bible, most supposedly ethical principles are not advocated for strictly moral considerations. Instead, they are a precondition for reward. The Beatitudes from the Sermon on the Mount (Matt. 5:3–10; Luke 6:17–26, incidentally, has it occur on a plain) are methods of getting something. The Beatitudes explain that those who are poor, who weep, who go hungry, and so on, will be rewarded. Those who are rich, well-fed, laugh, and those of whom others speak well will be punished, even though the latter class make it possible for the former class to exist. This is a system of scheming for motives of self-interest at the expense of others, not a system of ethics.

b. The bible often has vague principles.

Some principles mentioned in the bible are too vague to be of use in most circumstances; they can be interpreted in so many different ways that they are useless as guides to conduct.

(i) The "Love thy neighbor" principle is vague.

An example of a vague moral principle from the bible is *"Love thy neighbor as thyself"* (Matt. 22:39, Rom. 13:9, Gal. 5:14, and James 2:8).[4] Matthew 19:19 has Jesus list this principle along with others from the ten commandments, but it is actually from Leviticus 19:18.[5] But is this principle useful? Is it a good guide to conduct?

If my neighbor borrows my lawn mower and then does not return it after three years, should I let the neighbor keep it? Is that how I love myself? The principle is not clear. What of someone who is suicidal? Such a person loves himself or herself in such a way as to believe that death is preferable to life. Murder would be allowed in the case of such a person, since he or she would be loving others as that person loves himself or herself, but that is absurd. The principle is just too vague.

(ii) The "golden rule" is a vague principle.

What about the "golden rule": *"And as ye would that men should do to you, do ye also to them likewise"* (Luke 6:31)? It is not, of course, original with Christianity. Other religions, such as Buddhism, Confucianism, Hinduism, and the Jewish Talmud had such a rule much earlier. But is it a good principle? We have all met at least one person who boasts that he or she never accepted help from anyone in times of hardship and who thus, by the golden rule, can justify that he or she won't help anyone else. But not helping others who are

31

in need contradicts other ethical principles in the bible, such as that of giving your possessions to anyone who asks for something and lending to anyone who wants to borrow (Matt. 5:42, Luke 6:30).

Other examples of the shortcomings of this principle are easy to imagine. Suppose someone, call him Mr. Rugged, thinks that modern people are too comfortable. Mr. Rugged believes that people should not have air conditioners, cars, television, and other modern devices. Further, he holds that if he ever started to become soft, contented, then he would want someone to make sure he became toughened again. So, by the golden rule, he can justify vandalizing cars, destroying air conditioners, breaking computers, and other destructive acts, all done according to the golden rule.

Homosexuality is easily justified by this rule. A man who wants to have sex with someone obviously wants someone else to have sex with a man, and he wants this done to himself. However, if one should do to others what one wants done to oneself, then he should have sex with a man, too. Most Christians profess to be opposed to homosexuality, but the ambiguity of the golden rule permits it. In addition, some Southern slave owners thought: "If I belonged to an inferior race, I would want to be enslaved by a superior race, too, for my own good. I would get to be a part of a superior culture, and I would become a Christian." Thus was slavery "justified" by the golden rule. It is not clear whether this rule really prohibits many immoral actions. The golden rule is so vague it allows one to act in ways which contradict intuitive notions of right and wrong, as well as other principles expressed in the bible.

c. The bible has inadequate principles.

The bible has no advice about many modern problems. There is no direct reference to the issues of abortion, contraception, the distribution of limited supplies of organs from organ donors (who should get preference?), pollution, deforestation, overpopulation, corporate raiding, euthanasia, the right to privacy, patents, copyrights, and many other complex areas. If the bible is supposed to be used as *the* guide to moral conduct, it is woefully inadequate.

d. The bible recommends actions which are unethical!

Below are a few of the many principles in the bible which run contrary to common sense or intuitive notions of what is right and wrong.

(i) The bible says that one should not resist evil.

The bible reports Jesus as having said, *"But I say unto you, That ye resist not evil: but whosoever shall smite thee on they right cheek, turn to him the other also"* (Matt. 5:39). Does anyone really think that it would be wise to allow evil to reign unchecked? Should we get rid of our police force and our criminal justice system? If someone is trying to rape your daughter should you not interfere? If someone is stabbing your father should you do nothing? Surely this is bad advice.

Some commentators suggest that Jesus' precept only applies to oneself, that one could render aid to another but one could not help oneself if attacked or abused. Even if this is correct, this does not solve anything. If you go to the aid of someone who is being harmed, for example, and the attacker turns on you, then you would not be allowed to defend yourself. You would be unable to stop the attacker. At best you would be allowed to distract him or her by offering yourself as another victim. Imagine how much worse the world would be if those with malicious intent knew that their victims would not resist their efforts.

(ii) The bible is pro-slavery.

The Old Testament has a number of pro-slavery verses. Exodus 21:7 explains how a father is allowed to sell a daughter into slavery. Exodus 21:20 states explicitly that it is permissible to beat a slave to death as long as the slave does not die from the beating immediately. Leviticus 25:44 explains where to get slaves. There are scores of other such passages.

In the New Testament, Ephesians 6:5 tells slaves to obey their earthly masters as they would Christ, with sincerity of heart. Colossians 3:22 says the same thing. Titus 2:9 also tells slaves to obey their masters in everything and to try to please them, and 1 Peter 2:18 says the same thing about obeying harsh masters as well as good ones. In 1 Corinthians 7:21–24 Paul tells slaves that if they were "called" while a slave—that is, called to become Christians—then they should remain slaves and not try to be free. Paul says of remaining a slave, *"Don't let it trouble you"* (New International Version). The entire book called Philemon is a letter from Paul to a slave owner. Paul encountered the runaway slave Onesimus and was *sending him back to his owner!* Paul, of course, was aware that, upon receipt, the slave owner was legally obligated to either kill the slave or brand his forehead with an "F" for *Fugitivus*—"fugitive." Was Paul doing to another what he would have wanted done to himself?

There are many other unmistakably pro-slavery passages to be found in the bible. Some translations of the bible, such as the NIV, render the Greek word for slave, *doulos*, as "servant" to try to minimize the pro-slavery slant in the New Testament, but the bible is clearly pro-slavery. Jesus himself was well aware of slavery and even talked about slaves in parables. Now ask yourself: *why didn't Jesus condemn slavery?* How odd that Jesus got angry that people were changing money in a temple (Matt. 21:12, Mark 11:15), but he was obviously not angry about slavery. (And, incidentally, why

34

did Jesus chase out the people who were changing money in the temple? He said not to resist one who is evil [Matt. 5:39].)

(iii) Jesus was a racist.

When a foreign woman asked Jesus for help, he initially refused to help, or even to speak to her, because of her race. He explained this by referring to Gentiles as "dogs" (Matt. 15:21–28, Mark 7:25–30). Jesus also initially told his disciples not to go among the Gentiles (Matt. 10:5). He made it clear that he was only here for the "lost sheep of the house of Israel" (Matt. 15:24). Was Jesus loving his neighbor as he loved himself when he was being racist? Was he doing to them what he wanted done to himself?

These days compassionate people consider racism immoral.

(iv) The bible sometimes shows genocide as a moral duty.

Genesis 7: God commits genocide on an epic scale, killing everything on earth but Noah, his seven kin, and the animals. Children, babies, pregnant women, and everyone else drown. God does not set a good example of how one should treat others.

Deuteronomy 20:16: Moses tells his armies that, in the countries god is going to give them as inheritance, they are not allowed to leave alive anything that breathes. Joshua 10:40 reports that god also told Joshua to kill everything that breathes in neighboring regions, and he did. According to the bible, god made sure that the people in those areas could not negotiate for peace instead of being massacred. Joshua 11:20 states: *"For it was the LORD himself who hardened their hearts to wage war against Israel, so that he might destroy them totally, exterminating them without mercy, as the LORD had commanded Moses"* (NIV). This is reported in the bible again and again, this mass genocide on god's command.

In 1 Samuel 15:3 Samuel quotes to Saul the orders from god: *"Now go, attack the Amelekites and totally destroy everything that belongs to them. Do not spare them; put to death men and women, children and infants, cattle and sheep, camels and donkeys"* (NIV). Saul does not kill everything, however. He leaves the Amelekite leader and a few healthy animals alive so they can be sacrificed to god later. The bible tells us that, because of this, god "grieves" that he made Saul king because Saul did not carry out the instructions to the letter, and god sends someone to kill Saul (1 Sam. 28:18–19)! Here it is clear that genocide, wholesale slaughter, is a moral duty, inasmuch as failure to kill everything was punishable by god. Are we to believe the bible on this matter, that it is morally good to slaughter men, women, children, and infants without mercy?

(v) God punishes people by causing them to become cannibals.

The bible states in Leviticus 26:29 that those who do not listen to god will be punished in the following way: *"And ye shall eat the flesh of your sons, and the flesh of your daughters ye shall eat."* There are similar passages in Deuteronomy 28:53–57, Jeremiah 19:9, Lamentations 2:20, and Ezekiel 5:8–10. In 2 Kings 6:24–33 and Lamentations 4:10–11 we read that god has carried out his threat and has caused people to engage in cannibalism. Is that how others should be punished, by causing them to eat their innocent children?

(vi) The bible states that we should obey all governing authorities.

According to the bible, we should obey all rulers and civil authorities, and we should not resist their orders, *"for there is no authority except from God, and the authorities that exist are appointed by God. There-*

36

fore whoever resists the authority resists the ordinance of God, and those who resist will bring judgment on themselves" (Rom. 13:1–2 [New King James version (NKJ)]; see also Titus 3:1 and 1 Peter 2:13).[6]

Is this a good principle? Was it a moral duty for all Germans to rally behind Hitler simply because he was a governing authority? Was it, as the bible suggests, immoral to resist Hitler's orders to kill the millions sent to the death camps? Is the Rev. Martin Luther King Jr. suffering eternal agony because of his peaceful but sometimes illegal activities? Was Hitler appointed by the Christian god? Then so was Stalin, Mussolini, Pontius Pilate, and all other governing authorities. Surely this is nonsense.

(vii) The bible approves of kidnap and rape.

Numbers 31:7–15: Moses' army kills all the men of the Midianites. Moses is angry with his soldiers for allowing all of the women to live. He tells them to kill all the boys and all the women—except for the female virgins. These they can keep for themselves. They end up keeping 32,000 virgins, of whom thirty-two are given as tribute to the Lord, whatever that means. (Many scholars think that this means they were human sacrifices.) According to the bible, then, on god's authority, Moses tells his army to kill the men, women, and sons, and that they may rape the daughters.[7]

In Deuteronomy 21:10–14, Moses explains to his army that a kidnapped virgin is to be taken home, have her head shaved, her nails trimmed, and kept as a wife on a trial basis. If she is not satisfactory, she is to be released. Judges 21:10–24 tells of another two instances of kidnap and rape.

37

(viii) The bible sanctions the murder of civilians during wartime.

Apart from deliberate genocide, the killing of civilians during wartime was also god's will, according to the bible. Isaiah 13 tells of a prophecy regarding Babylon. We find in verse 16 what will happen when its inhabitants fall prey to the "wrath of the Lord Almighty": *"Their infants will be dashed to pieces before their eyes; their houses looted and their wives ravished."* And verse 18: *"Their bows will strike down the young men; they will have no mercy on infants nor will they look with compassion on children"* (NIV). Compare Hosea 13:16's prophesy regarding the Samarians: *"They shall fall by the sword; their infants shall be dashed in pieces, and their women with child shall be ripped up."* There are many other verses of the bible which show a complete disregard for the value of human life.

(ix) The bible endorses the oppression of women.

Those who oppress women have long been able to rely on the bible as a sanction. In addition to the examples of biblical passages which approve of the kidnapping and raping of young women, there are other verses which also disparage women. Genesis 3:16 states that the husband shall rule over the wife. This is reiterated in 1 Corinthians 11:3, Ephesians 5:22–24, 1 Peter 3:1–7, and implicit in scores of other passages. First Corinthians 14:34–35 states that women are not to speak in church; if a woman has a question, she must ask her husband at home. First Timothy 2:11–14 says that a woman is not to teach or have any authority over the man. The reason for this is that it was Eve who was deceived and sinful, not Adam. Because Eve was deceived before Adam, women have often been considered temptresses in the eyes of the Church.

The bible implies that childbirth is a sin. Leviticus 12:2–4 states that a woman who bears a son is unclean for seven days and must continue with purification for thirty-three days, and Leviticus 12:5 states that a woman who bears a daughter is unclean for fourteen days and must continue with purification for sixty-six days. Apparently it is twice as sinful to bear a daughter as it is to bear a son. After giving birth, a woman must give a burnt offering and a sin offering as atonement (Lev. 12:6–7). What does one atone for but sin? The words translated as "clean" and "unclean" from the Hebrew do not refer to hygiene, scholars tell us, but to one's relationship to the divine. Luke 2:22, incidentally, shows that Mary was unclean after the birth of Jesus.

Leviticus 19:20–21 explains that if a master has sex with a female slave who is engaged to someone else, *she* is punished but the man may be forgiven. Deuteronomy 22:23–24 states that if a woman betrothed to a man is raped in the city, both she and her rapist are to be stoned to death. If she is raped in the country, only the rapist is killed. However, if she is not engaged to be married, according to Deuteronomy 22:28–29, she must marry her rapist. Numbers 5:11–31 has an agonizing adulteress test. Men are not tested. Deuteronomy 22:13–21 has a barbaric virgin test for women. The tenth commandment (Exod. 20:17, Deut. 5:21) calls a wife a husband's possession and lists her along with an ox and an ass.

These days, compassionate men and women believe that men and women should be considered equals.

Perhaps now the Christian should be asked: if the bible is so wrong about such issues as racism, slavery, kidnapping, rape, genocide, and so forth, *why should anyone trust it to be a reliable guide to morality in other areas?* Perhaps Thomas Paine, one of our founding fathers, made the point best in *The Age of Reason*:

Whenever we read the obscene stories, the voluptuous debaucheries, the cruel and tortuous executions, the unrelenting vindictiveness with which more than half the Bible is filled, it would be more consistent that we call it the word of a demon than the word of God. It is a history of wickedness that has served to corrupt and brutalize mankind; and, for my part, I sincerely detest it, as I detest everything that is cruel.[8]

There are many other verses of the bible which advocate principles and conduct which people of conscience would consider immoral, far too many to include here. Here is an interesting thought experiment: If you had gone into one of those regions and had watched soldiers kill babies, rip open pregnant women, and rape young girls, would you have been able to place your hand on your heart and *honestly* say, "This was commanded by the god of love and peace" (as he is called in 2 Cor. 13:11)? Surely this is absurd. Is this really the sort of ethics which might be the product of divine omniscience and omnibenevolence? Ask yourself: could the commands of a demon be any worse?

e. The bible contains contradictory ethical views.

Another important part of why the bible is inadequate as a foundation is that it contains so many contradictory principles and examples of hypocrisy. Below are a few of these.

(i) Should we love our enemies?

We should love our enemies and do good to those who hate us, according to Matthew 5:44, Luke 6:27, and Luke 6:35. But the bible is not consistent about how one's enemies should be treated.

(A) According to the bible, Jesus contradicted the "love your enemies" principle by saying that all those who are not for him are against him (Matt. 12:30). Those who are against him are his enemies. Thus, he should love those who are against him. But he did

40

not. Jesus made it clear that those who were not his followers would be sent to hell. There are numerous instances of this sort of thinking in the bible, such as Matthew 13:41–42, 49–50, and other verses. Is this love for one's enemies? Of course not. *You don't send those you love to eternal torture.* That's not doing good to one who hates you. If Jesus would send his enemies to hell, he certainly doesn't love them, and thus he violates his own teaching. If, on this view, one can love another person and still send that person to hell forever, then love means nothing in the Christian perspective.

(B) Many examples in the bible suggest that one ought to slaughter those who are not on god's side. Obviously, all the passages cited above about butchering enemies would contradict the principle of loving your enemies and doing good to those who hate you. In many cases the bible says specifically that god orders his enemies massacred. For example, Exodus 32:25–28: Moses caught his people running wild and worshiping a golden calf. God tells Moses to gather together those who are still on his side, on god's side. Moses does this, and he then tells the loyal ones to go through the camp and kill their own brothers and sisters, children and parents, friends and neighbors, or anyone else who is not on god's side. According to the bible, they kill about three thousand people. Moses tells his followers, *"You have been set apart to the Lord today, for you were against your own sons and brothers, and he has blessed you this day"* (Exod. 32:29 [NIV]). Interestingly, Moses' brother Aaron, who made the golden calf, is not punished.

Thus, the bible gives contradictory views about how one should treat one's enemies.

(ii) Is it immoral to call someone else an insulting name?

Jesus told his followers that anyone who calls someone else a fool is in danger of hell fire (Matt. 5:22). Colossians 3:8 states: *"But now you must rid yourselves of all such things as these: anger, rage, malice, slander, and filthy language from your lips."* The intent of these passages is surely that calling other people insulting names is forbidden.

However, Jesus, who supposedly lived a perfect life (1 Pet. 2:21–22), called people fools (Matt. 23:17, Luke 11:40). He called the Pharisees names such as hypocrites (Matt. 15:7, 22:18, 23:15, 23, 27, 29 and other verses); a generation of vipers, snakes, and a brood of vipers (Matt. 12:34, 23:33); blind, blind guides, blind fools (Matt. 15:14, 23:16,17, 26); and a tomb full of dead bones (Matt. 23:27). And there are other examples.

Jesus called people insulting names. Clearly, the bible gives contradictory views about the moral status of name-calling.

(iii) Is lying immoral?

Jesus told his followers that lying is evil (Matt. 15:19, Mark 7:22). Proverbs 6:17–19 tells us that god hates a lying tongue and a false witness.

However, according to the bible itself, Jesus was sometimes dishonest. During his hearing before the high priest, Jesus says, *"I spoke openly to the world. I always taught in synagogues and in the temple, where the Jews always meet, and in secret I have said nothing"* (John 18:20 [NKJ]). Other parts of the Bible show that this is false. Jesus did not always teach in synagogues and temples. He taught on a mountain (Matt. 5:1–2), on a boat (Matt. 13:1–35), on a plain (Luke 6:17–49), and other places. And did he say things in secret? He told his followers that he spoke in parables so that those who were not part of his group would not be able to understand his teaching, *"So that, 'they may be ever seeing but never perceiving, and ever hearing but never understanding; otherwise they might turn and be forgiven!'"* (Mark 4:12 [NIV]). Matthew 13:11–15 says the same thing. Jesus admits that he used parables so that the meaning of his stories would remain a secret to most of his audience, *"But when he was alone with his own disciples, he explained everything"* (Mark 4:34 [NIV]). Many other passages, such as Matthew 13:36–52 and Luke 18:34, show Jesus taking his disciples aside to tell them something in secret. Jesus was dishonest in denying that he said things in secret and in stating that he taught only in the synagogues and in the temple.

Here's another example of a lie told by Jesus. Having been invited to go to the Feast of the Tabernacles in Jerusalem, he told his followers, *"You go up to this feast. I am not going up to this feast, for my time has not yet fully come"* (John 7:8 [NKJ]). But after his followers left Jesus went up to the feast *"not openly, but as it were, in secret"* (John 7:10). This caused people there to complain about Jesus and say that he *"deceives the people"* (John 7:12), which, according to the bible, was true. Note that some versions of the bible insert the word "yet" between "not" and "going" in John 7:8 to suggest that Jesus was actually saying that he was "not yet going" to the feast, with the possibility that he would go later. The word "yet" was added by a copyist sometime long after the writing of John to try to make it seem that Jesus was not lying. The word is missing from early manuscripts of the book, so scholars know that it does not belong there. Some of the more scholarly versions of the bible will concede this in a footnote. Clearly, Jesus was not always honest.

An amusing case of Jesus' fibbing occurs in Luke 23:39–43. One of the robbers crucified with Jesus insults him, and the other criminal rebukes the first, stating that Jesus has done nothing wrong. Jesus tells this criminal, *"I tell you the truth, today you will be with me in paradise"* (Luke 23:43 [NIV]). However, when he died, Jesus supposedly descended into hell (Acts 2:31). This has led some commentators to remark that, if the story is true, that was one very surprised thief![9]

There are many other examples of divine lying and deception

in the bible, including examples of god himself causing people to believe lies. For example, 2 Thessalonians 2:11–12 states that god *"shall send them strong delusion, that they should believe a lie: That they all might be damned who believed not the truth. . . ."* If god causes people to believe lies so that he can send them to hell, this not only contradicts the notion that god abhors lies, it shows that the god of the bible is not omnibenevolent. Surely it is incompatible with being all-good to force someone to believe something which results in that person being punished. This is also at odds with 1 Timothy 2:3–4, which states that god *"wants all men to be saved and to come to a knowledge of the truth"* (NIV). Does the god of the bible want all people to know the truth and be saved or does he want some to believe lies and be damned? One of these verses, or both of them, *must* be false.

First Kings 22:20–23 also shows god endorsing outright lying. Verse 23 states: *"Now therefore, behold, the LORD hath put a lying spirit in the mouth of all these thy prophets, and the LORD hath spoken evil concerning thee."* This is repeated in 2 Chronicles 18:22. Ezekiel 14:9 says: *"And if the prophet be deceived when he hath spoken a thing, I the LORD have deceived that prophet. . . ."* Interestingly, in the latter case, the bible states that the punishment for false prophesy will be death even though the prophet was deceived by god himself! Again, this is hardly compatible with omnibenevolence.

Ezekiel 20:25–26 states that god intentionally gave his people bad laws, including those which required the sacrifice of their firstborn children, in order to fill them with horror so that they would know that he is the lord. Is it compatible with being omnibenevolent to cause people to sacrifice children so that they can know that god is powerful? Could little children who are sacrificed benefit from such a law? And is that how one knows that god is at work in the world, when one is filled with horror? If god sometimes gives people laws which he knows are bad, which are calculated to

44

fill people with horror and not to make them better or moral, then god cannot be trusted to be forthright and honest about explaining our moral duties. If god has lied in the past about whether some laws are moral, then one can never be certain that laws which are supposedly from god now are moral.

Jesus and god are supposed to be morally perfect, yet the bible shows them engaged in deception. The bible thus gives contradictory views about the moral status of lying. More importantly, the bible shows god and Jesus to be unreliable sources of moral laws because they are not honest.

(iv) Should we honor our parents?

Exodus 20:12 and Deuteronomy 5:16, as part of the ten commandments,[10] state: *"honor thy father and thy mother."* Jesus endorses this commandment in Matthew 15:4 and 19:19, Mark 7:10–13, Mark 10:19, and Luke 18:20.

Yet Jesus said, *"If anyone comes to me and does not hate his father and mother, his wife and children, his brothers and sisters—yes, even his own life—he cannot be my disciple"* (Luke 14:26 [NIV]). Regarding this passage, in *The Perfect Mirror? The Question of Bible Perfection,* author Darrel Henschell comments on the Greek word *miseo* which is translated as "hate":

> The word "hate" is retained in this verse by all . . . major translations. . . . Also, the Greek word translated as "hate" here is the exact same word that is translated as "hate" in these scriptures: John 3:20; 7:7; 15:18; 1 John 3:13.[11]

Obviously one who hates his or her parents does not honor them. It would seem that in order to be a disciple of Jesus one must break one of the ten commandments. Curiously, 1 John 4:20 states: *"If anyone says, 'I love God,' yet hates his brother, he is a liar,"* and 1 John 3:5 holds that *"anyone who hates his brother is a murderer"* (NIV)! It would seem that one may have to break at least three commandments in order to follow Jesus. How odd, in any case, that the biblical Jesus wanted us to love those who hate us and hate those who love us. Does that seem like a good idea? Are these the good, wholesome family values which the clergy tell us we can find in the bible?

Furthermore, the bible also shows Jesus speaking harshly to his mother, Mary, at the wedding in Cana (John 2:4), and when he was only twelve years old he scolded her when she asked him why he had been missing for three days in the city (Luke 2:49). He also addressed her as "woman" twice (John 2:4 and 19:26). These things certainly do not seem respectful. The bible has no record of Jesus once speaking kindly to his mother. Matthew 23:9 has Jesus say not to call any man on earth "father." The bible does not record Jesus *ever* speaking to Joseph, his father. Jesus is never described honoring his father or mother.

Clearly, the bible gives contradictory answers to the question of whether we should respect our parents. On these ethical issues, and many others, the bible gives contradictory advice.

3. Objections to the above critique of theistic ethics fail.

Below are a few of the common objections to an attack upon Christian ethics and theistic ethics. None of the objections is successful.

a. Can't the Christian just reject certain parts of the bible and keep others? Can't he or she reject the "bad" parts and keep the "moral" parts?

Why would someone adopt a book such as the bible for a supposed source of moral teaching when most of the ethics in the book have to be ignored? How would you respond to a Nazi who used Hitler's *Mein Kampf* as a guide to ethics and then replied to your objections that the immoral parts should be rejected? If a book is filled with immorality, if many of its main characters are bloodthirsty butchers, why would someone who disagrees with such a view use that book as a guide to morality?

If one accepts parts of the bible and rejects others, this is admitting that the bible is an inadequate guide to morality. If one picks and chooses from the bible, then one needs to be able to recognize what is moral and what is not before beginning the selection process. To do this, one must have a nonbiblical source of morality which determines what to pick and what to reject. Perhaps one has a gut feeling about what is right and wrong. Call it moral intuition, human compassion, whatever. One may even have some abstract, philosophical theory of ethics which allows one to decide which biblical precepts are morally acceptable. A person who uses these sources as guides to morality apparently thinks that his or her own gut feeling or moral system is a better guide to morality than the bible and thus would have to admit that the bible is an inadequate source for morality.

If one already has a biblically independent source of morality, and parts of the bible must be denounced as immoral, of what use is the bible for morality? It plays no role in forming the ethical view. It is merely being used to ease the conscience of the person who does not want to admit that his or her moral view is not based on the bible. Picking and choosing from the bible, rather than defending the bible as an adequate source of morals, admits defeat!

b. Can't the Christian just claim that god will guide him or her through prayer or by some sort of feeling about what it is right to do?

A quick look at human history, or even at the bible, shows what atrocities have been committed by those who thought that they were guided by god. The Spanish inquisitions, the slaughter of Jews by Christians during the Crusades, John Calvin's reign of terror in Geneva all shed a great deal of blood and unleashed the most sadistic impulses of the human heart, and all were the products of those who thought that they had been guided by god's inspiration. It seems unlikely that relying on prayer or other vague criteria could serve as an adequate basis for morality. However, there are more specific responses to the notion of being guided by prayer.

(i) If one appeals to "feelings," and not reasons, then there is no clear way to tell whether someone, even oneself, has been guided by god. The Christian can never condemn another's actions, even the slaughter of infants or the torture of children, if the person performing the act simply makes the claim that god is on his or her side. Anything is then permitted, and it would not be difficult to cite biblical passages to "justify" anything from rape to infanticide. Because there is no way to distinguish between being inspired by god and *mistakenly thinking* that one is inspired by god, claims that one is inspired by god are worthless.

(ii) Christians have incompatible claims that they are inspired by god. Baptists disagree with Catholics, Seventh-day Adventists disagree with Lutherans, and so on, yet members of each claim to be inspired, guided, by god. Again, since there is no criterion for morality used other than the mere assertion of inspiration itself, there is no way in practice to distinguish between the "true" claims and the false ones. So the claims are useless.

(iii) Another problem is that those of other religions also appeal to the same "feeling" or response to prayer, yet the Christian does not believe the claims of other religions. This shows that not even the Christian believes that an appeal to "inspiration" is sufficient justification for conduct.

(iv) Finally, as noted above, the Euthyphro dilemma shows that the divine command theory of ethics, the view that god is the source of morality, does not serve as an adequate foundation for morality.

c. How can the atheist say that the bible recommends immoral actions and principles? What standard is the atheist using?

Sometimes Christians retort that one cannot condemn the atrocities of the bible because one would need another moral system in order to condemn them. To this there are two responses:

(i) Some Christians have actually tried to tell me that going into a neighboring region and slaughtering anything that breathes is not immoral, that slavery is not immoral, that kidnap and rape are not immoral, and so on. To such people I have this to say: it is *your* so-called system of ethics which is deplorable, not mine. If you can't see that these actions are immoral, then it is *you* who are living unfettered by a moral system, not me. Even if the atheist did not have a well-developed system of ethics with which to condemn the atrocities described in the bible, surely one could still say that a system of ethics is designed to allow one to denounce exactly those sorts of actions which I have presented from the bible. If any and all of those horrible acts described above are permitted on the Christian view, then *what is it that you can't do on that "morality"?* What is the point of claiming that you have an ethical system if anything is permitted? As I have noted above, the defense of such horrible conduct reduces Christian ethics to a system of slavery, of

49

obedience, instead of a system of morality. Such a view makes a mockery of the concept of ethics.

(ii) There are many powerful systems of ethics which can be used to condemn the atrocities of the bible, and none of these systems requires belief in gods. That is the subject of the next section.

Summary of section A

The preceding section has covered a lot of material, so before proceeding to the next section a brief review might be helpful.

I have argued that theism is an inadequate source of morality because it posits a deity as the source of ethics. This divine command theory of ethics is so riddled with problems, both theoretical and practical, that it is indefensible. Below is a list of the main points of my argument.

1. The Euthyphro dilemma is conclusive against the view that god is the source of morality.
2. The bible is inadequate as a source of morality.
   a) It is not clear that many principles in the bible are intended to be ethical.
   b) The bible gives vague moral guidelines.
   c) The bible gives inadequate moral guidelines.
   d) The bible recommends actions which are immoral.
   e) The bible contains contradictory ethical views.
3. Objections to the analysis above fail.

Therefore, the view that god is the source of morality is untenable.

Demonstrating the failure of theistic ethics lessens the burden on the atheist with respect to morality. Even if atheism were incompatible with having an ethical system, the fact that theism is insufficient to ground morality would simply put both views on even ground. Any possibility of a moral foundation on the atheistic view would give that view a clear advantage where morals are concerned. To this task we now turn.

B. There are many powerful ethical systems which do not require belief in gods.

Throughout human history, theists, atheists, and agnostics have recognized that the divine command theory of ethics does not work and that holy books such as the bible cannot serve as adequate foundations for morality. As a result, many philosophers have developed complex and intellectually powerful systems of ethics which do not rely on the concept of god in any way. Even some theists who have recognized the failure of the divine command theory of ethics have subscribed to some of these views. Because of the complexity of these moral systems, they cannot be explained in great detail here. However, because many people have never heard of ethical systems which do not require god, a *brief* summation of some of the most important features of these systems is provided below.

Remember that these are not "atheist" ethics, as if all atheists adhere to any one of these views. They are, instead, moral systems which can function in the absence of belief in god. I will briefly describe Kant's ethical theory, utilitarianism, and virtue-based systems.

1. *Kant's ethical theory does not require god.*

Immanuel Kant (1724–1804) was extremely influential in the development of many areas of philosophy. His immense *Critique of Pure Reason*, published in 1781, changed the way philosophers examined the nature of human knowledge. His booklet, *Groundwork for the Metaphysics of Morals*, published in 1785, was influential in the field of ethics.[12]

Kant thought that the only thing that could be called good unconditionally is a good will. In other words, it is not what we do which makes us morally good or bad, it is what we intend to do and what we attempt to accomplish. For example, if a conscientious lifeguard, Jones, does his best to save Smith from drowning, but fails, we would not say that Jones is a bad person simply because the results were undesirable. Even though Jones failed, Jones acted according to what was morally required: he attempted to save the person's life. What is important is one's motive.

Suppose two couples on a date walk past a person asking for a handout. One of the two in the first couple thinks, "This poor soul is in need. I haven't given to the poor for a while. I should do so now," and gives the beggar some money. However, the man in the next couple sees that same beggar and thinks, "It is a shame that society allows such filth to walk the streets, but perhaps I can use this opportunity to my advantage. I will give this eyesore some money. I think this will impress my date and land me in bed with her. It's worth parting with the money," and gives the beggar the same amount of money as the person from the first couple. Surely there is some moral difference between these actions, although the two people gave the same amount of money to the same person. The difference seems to be the motive for the actions. On Kant's view, as long as one is acting out of respect for the moral law, and not out of selfishness, for example, then one is acting morally. But how does one determine the moral law, one's moral duty?

Kant distinguished between two kinds of commands or imperatives. Some are called hypothetical; that is, they depend on some further goal in order to have any force. For example, the statement "If you want to get a good grade on the test, then you should study hard for the test tomorrow" is based on the assumption that the person addressed wants to get a good grade on the test. If he or she does not want to get a good grade, then the "should" in the command has no force. Similarly, if I do not care if I have bad health or a flabby physique, then the command "You should exercise regularly" has no force. Kant held that commands of this kind are not ethical commands.

On the other hand, Kant argues, there are other commands such as "You should not steal" or "You should keep promises" which do not rest on additional assumptions or goals. These kinds of commands apply regardless of the particular circumstances or desires of the person in question. These commands have force because to violate them is to contradict oneself.

For example, suppose that Ms. Johnson wonders whether it is morally permissible to steal. She wants to act according to the maxim, the principle of action, that stealing is permissible. According to Kant, there is a way to find out whether acting according to this motive is moral or not. It requires a thought experiment, an exercise in the imagination. Ms. Johnson needs to "universalize" the principle; that is, she must imagine that *everyone* else also accepts the principle that stealing is permitted and then examine the result. What is the result? Well, Ms. Johnson could imagine that she may calmly walk to the local jewelry store and leave with a free handful of gems. In her thought experiment this would be all right, since everyone agrees that stealing is fine. But her neighbor may also want gems and would be free to come over to Ms. Johnson's house and take them. Ms. Johnson would not object, since everyone in this thought experiment, including herself, agrees that stealing is permitted. Perhaps another person may then steal the gems from the neighbor, and then the store owner may steal them back, and so on. What has happened here? The gems are changing hands, but since each person agrees that the next person has the right to take the gems, *they are no longer stealing.* The concept of ownership and personal property becomes vacuous, and taking another person's property without permission becomes impossible, since they all give such permission. Thus, universalizing the maxim that stealing is permitted has resulted in a contradiction. It can't be the case that everyone is permitted to steal, since the result would be that no one could possibly steal. On Kant's view, this shows that stealing is not permitted. The maxim that stealing is permitted results in contradiction, and a contradiction is always, by definition, false. Thus, it *must* be false that stealing is permitted, so to act according to that maxim is immoral. What Kant's strategy shows, then, is that if the maxim one wishes to use as a principle of action cannot be universalized, then acting according to that maxim is immoral.

Kant believed that many other moral duties were discoverable in this way, by checking for contradictions when universalized. For example, Kant explained how he could derive moral duties prohibiting suicide, requiring one to give to the needy, requiring one to keep promises, and many others. Kant also held that each person should treat the other as an "end," as another moral being whose goals and interests are no less legitimate than one's own.

For Kant, the cornerstone of ethics is the recognition of the categorical imperative, a command which, unlike the hypothetical ones, holds under all circumstances. Kant explains the categorical imperative:

Act only according to that maxim whereby you can at the same
time will that it should become a universal law.[13]

This categorical imperative serves as an objective, impartial test for
morality. One's own desires and needs do not affect the laws of
logic. The categorical imperative is, in the end, an unbiased test for
logical contradiction. Its force is the power of reason itself. The fact
that an immoral maxim is contradictory proves that it *must* be false.

If one defines an objective moral value as one in which individual wishes or goals are irrelevant to the force or truth of that
moral value, then clearly Kant's moral theory produces objective
moral values—without appeal to god or any supernatural guidance.

Sometimes theists try to suggest that Kant thought that morality
required a god in order to make sense or to have force. Kant was
adamant that morality is definitely *not* in any way founded on the
will of a deity but instead rests on pure reason. Kant wrote:

> So far as morality is based upon the conception of man as a free
> agent who, just because he is free, binds himself through his
> reason to unconditioned laws, it stands in need neither of the
> idea of another Being over him, for him to apprehend his duty,
> nor of an incentive other than the law itself, for him to do his
> duty. At least it is man's own fault if he is subject to such a need;
> and if he is, this need can be relieved through nothing outside
> himself: for whatever does not originate in himself and his own
> freedom in no way compensates for the deficiency of his
> morality. Hence for its own sake morality does not need religion
> at all . . . ; by virtue of pure practical reason it is self-sufficient.[14]

In fact, Kant thought that anyone who needs some ulterior end or
motive to act according to the moral law is contemptible.[15] Getting
into heaven or avoiding hell would be examples of ulterior motives.

There is, of course, much more to Kant's view, and modern-day scholars who endorse and elaborate on Kant's ethics have continued to defend their position from criticism and have made the contemporary Kantian moral theory even more powerful and robust than the original.

2. Mill's utilitarian system of ethics does not require god.

The English philosopher and jurist Jeremy Bentham (1748–1832) developed a moral theory known as utilitarianism, of which there are many versions. The influential philosopher, social critic, and economist John Stuart Mill (1806–1873) popularized and defended Bentham's view in his book *Utilitarianism,* published in 1861.

The principle of utility, which Bentham called the "greatest happiness" principle, is the foundation of the utilitarian system. Mill explains:

> The creed which accepts as the foundation of morals "utility" or the "greatest happiness principle" holds that actions are right in proportion as they tend to promote happiness, wrong as they tend to produce the reverse of happiness.[16]

The utilitarian view, then, advocates that, when faced with the various choices in life, one should choose to perform those actions which promote the greatest amount of happiness in comparison with the other possible choices, or, if no choices cause any happiness, one should choose those actions which allow the least amount of pain. Of course, this does *not* mean that one would choose these actions with an eye toward how much happiness or unhappiness is caused only for oneself. On the utilitarian moral theory, one's own happiness and unhappiness do not play any more prominent a role in one's decisions than the happiness or unhappiness of any other person.

The different versions of utilitarianism use a variety of definitions of "happiness" and "unhappiness" (or "the reverse of happiness"), but on Mill's version "happiness" and "unhappiness" mean pleasure and pain, respectively. Mill believed that pleasure and freedom from pain are the only things desirable in themselves. It seems, he said, that anything else we desire is desired only for the sake of the pleasure that it brings or for its role in promoting pleasure or causing freedom from pain.[17]

Perhaps an example would be useful. Suppose that two college students, Carol and Penelope, live together in Penelope's large, expensive apartment. Penelope lets Carol live in her apartment rent free because their parents are old friends. Suppose further that, one day in March, Carol finds out that her friend and roommate Penelope has stolen a car in order to drive to South Padre Island during spring break. If Carol is a utilitarian, she will consider the effects of her possible courses of action. Suppose, for simplicity, that her options are that she may tell the police or she may keep quiet about the whole affair. If she tells the police about Penelope's theft, she risks losing both Penelope's friendship and the rent-free use of the apartment. On the other hand, if she says nothing about it to anyone, a great deal of unhappiness will befall the car's owner and, perhaps, the owner's spouse, children, insurance agency, and others. Carol realizes that her own unhappiness caused by the loss of a friend and the use of an apartment, as well as Penelope's unhappiness caused by imprisonment, would be outweighed by the unhappiness that would result if she kept quiet, and she decides to report the crime to the authorities. Although this results in Carol's own unhappiness, the utilitarian calculus has shown Carol her moral duty, and she performs it.

The idea that as one goes through life, and one is faced with a number of moral choices, that one should choose to perform those actions which make the world a better place for people by causing more happiness than unhappiness, that one should not simply choose what would make oneself happy at the expense of others, is an approach to life and morality that many people find intuitively satisfying. Mill, and others, have thought that such a life, a life of "few and transitory pains," and "many and various pleasures" was a real possibility and that the only hindrances to such a life being available to everyone were the "present wretched education and wretched social arrangements."[18]

The utilitarian theory of ethics produces objective moral values. Mill's short work *Utilitarianism* explains many advantages of his moral system, and it defends his view against various objections. Utilitarians of today have taken Mill's initial insights, and have, in the light of the objections and critiques of other philosophers, molded utilitarianism into a formidable ethical theory.

3. Virtue-based systems of ethics do not require god.

The ethical views which are subsumed under the name of "virtue-based" systems, sometimes called "aretaic" ethics (from the Greek *aretē*, or "virtue"), are part of a philosophical and ethical tradition which dates back as far as 300 B.C.E. or so with Aristotle.

While many other ethical systems focus on the rightness or wrongness of a particular action or class of actions, virtue-based theories focus on the character of the agent, the person making the choices. Virtue-based ethics promotes certain character traits, the "virtues," in the belief that the central issue of morality is not what sorts of actions are best, but what type of character, and what kind of life, is best. After all, if a society can promote the development of good moral character in its citizens, then there will no longer be a concern over whether people will choose the right actions instead of the wrong ones. Virtue-based ethics addresses the motivational and communal dimensions of ethical conduct, not just the rule-making aspect.

In *The Greek Way,* noted scholar Edith Hamilton explains what character meant to the Greeks of the ancient world:

> To us a man's character is peculiarly his own; it distinguishes each one from the rest. To the Greeks it was a man's share in qualities all men partake of; it united each one to the rest. We are interested in people's special characteristics, the things in this or that person which are different from the general. The Greeks, on the contrary, thought what was important in a man were precisely the qualities he shared with all mankind.[19]

The Greeks saw each individual as a part of the whole community, not as an isolated unit. Their approach to ethics reflects this emphasis, and it is evident in virtue-based ethics.

Aristotle explains that moral virtue, also called moral excellence, is "a state of character concerned with choice, lying in a mean. . . ."[20] The state of character is instilled by habit.[21] Society works to instill in its young citizens the habitual practice of responding with the appropriate action to situations which require moral choice. The "mean" refers to the state of character which does not respond with an inappropriate extreme in a given situation. For example, it is appropriate to give to the needy, but it would be a mistake to give *all* one has at every opportunity, since then one would be needy as well and nothing would have been solved. Although giving away all that one has may be appropriate in some situations, it is clearly not appropriate in all. A state of character which responds appropriately to the situation is, according to Aristotle, the best state of character, but it must also be informed by *phronesis,* or practical wisdom. Practical wisdom is the ability of a person to decide the appropriate action in a given circumstance.

But what are the appropriate actions? What should one do in a given situation? The virtue theorist might say that such questions are to some extent misguided. Virtue-based ethics are systems which recognize that the command or legalistic model of ethics is inadequate. Even if it were possible to construct a long list of commands to cover every possible situation (and a brief stroll through a law library should be enough to show that this is a daunting task), it would be impossible for anyone to memorize such a lengthy array of "moral laws" in order to put them to use.

The virtues which usually serve as the basis for a virtue-ethics system are well known. In *Forbidden Fruit: The Ethics of Humanism,* Paul Kurtz lists what he calls the "common moral decencies": integrity, including truthfulness, promise-keeping, sincerity, and honesty; trustworthiness, including fidelity and dependability; benevolence, including good will, refraining from harming others, respecting the property of others, sexual consent, and beneficence; and fairness, including gratitude, accountability, justice, tolerance, and cooperation.[22] Many philosophers have held that the value of such character traits is self-evident. No justification of such moral values is needed.

Virtue ethicists hold that the Greeks were wise in recognizing that it is more practical to attempt to instill in people a character which is the source of correct moral choices than to have every person memorize a long list of laws. Each situation demanding a moral choice is unique. A person who has a character which exemplifies honesty, fairness, gratitude, kindness, patience, and the other virtues, and who has a good dose of practical wisdom, is more likely to respond in a morally appropriate way to a given situation than someone who is greedy, selfish, cruel, and dishonest, and who has merely been given a long list of laws and a host of threats. Which type of person would you rather have for a neighbor?

Of course, Aristotle and other virtue-based ethical theorists do give specific, practical advice, but the emphasis is upon the person, not the law. Virtue-based ethical theories are comprehensive explanations of what it is to be moral. They address the role of the individual in society, morally appropriate action, the ideal kind of life for humans, and many other basic issues which are related to ethics but which are outside the scope of many other moral theories. Without a proper understanding of how these areas are related, according to virtue-based theorists, one cannot have a true understanding of the nature of morality and proper conduct.

Many bible scholars and theologians, as well as nonbelievers, have noted that the ethics of the bible, and especially of the Old Testament, entirely neglect the development of good moral character. A shallow, slave-master attitude toward being moral is what is promoted instead. All too often, being obedient is considered equivalent to being moral. Perhaps a good dose of virtue ethics would be a welcome change in many theists' households.

Summary of section B

Kant's ethical theory, Mill's utilitarianism, and the virtue-based theories of ethics are widely recognized to be important and influential contributions to moral philosophy, and none of them requires a god as a foundation. Remember also that there are other ethical theories which do not require god in order to function. The three views briefly explained above are just a few of the many theories and types of theories available, each of which is far superior to the divine command theory.

Conclusion

A. Theism is an inadequate foundation for morality.
B. There are many powerful systems of ethics which do not require belief in gods.

Therefore, the charge that the atheist cannot have a system of morals is groundless.

In order to show that the nontheistic ethical systems described above are inadequate, the theist must show that either: (a) the theistic moral system works, and that it contains some morally important element(s) which these nontheistic systems lack; and/or (b) the systems listed above, and others which do not require god, cannot serve as foundations to morality due to some other inherent flaw. No theist has ever been able to show either (a) or (b).

Many Christian apologists (defenders) endorse an argument, often called *the moral argument for god's existence*, which takes the following form:

1. If god does not exist, then there are no objective moral values.
2. There are objective moral values.

---

3. Therefore, god exists.

The argument is unsuccessful, however, because, as noted above, the Euthyphro dilemma makes the connection between god and moral values, a connection implied by premise (1) of the moral argument, extremely problematic for the theist. To show the truth of the first premise of the argument, the theist must show that morality is dependent on god, which is the position which the Euthyphro dilemma shows to be untenable. No theist has ever been able to support premise (1) effectively. Furthermore, since objective moral values can be produced by the systems of Kant and Mill independently of god, premise (1) can be shown to be false. Finally, the structure of the argument is such that, if the theist wishes to show that premise (2) is true, the existence of objective moral values must be demonstrated. However, this must be done without appealing to the concept of god, since it is the existence of god which is the conclusion of the argument. Any appeal to god in the premises would render the argument circular and useless. The theist must show, then, that objective moral values exist independently of showing that god exists, a feat which may be impossible without undermining premise (1). The moral argument is easily dismissed.

Theists today often bemoan the seeming decay of moral values in our society. Crime is rampant, and people are generally less concerned with the welfare of others than they seem to have been in generations past. The reasons for this are, of course, complex, but the theists themselves should be ready to take their share of the blame. For ages the clergy have been drumming into people's heads the idea that "without god there is no ethics," and yet they are unable to produce evidence for their god and claims about god's will. Thus, they are unable to produce what they insist is the foundation of ethics. The public, then, takes the clergy at their word and believes that there is no demonstrable foundation for ethics. Fortunately, however, as we have seen, ethics can be established without appeal to gods. In fact, given the atrocities that have been committed in the name of god, it is surprising that theists still have the audacity to suggest that god is the foundation of morality.

Notes

1. Just as "Dictionary" is capitalized only when it is in a title because there are many different dictionaries, "bible" should be capitalized only when it is used in a title because there are many different bibles, and not all of them are religious works.

2. See Plato, *The Euthyphro, Apology, Crito,* and *Phaedo,* Benjamin Jowett trans. (Amherst, N.Y.: Prometheus Books, 1988). Socrates and Euthyphro debate using terms such as "piety" and "holiness." However, modern readers may better appreciate the value of the dialogue with the substitution of different terms, such as "good" where Plato has "holy" and "commanded by god" where Plato has "beloved by the gods." This brings out the importance of the discussion in the held of ethics, and it is with this revised terminology that contemporary philosophers discuss the Euthyphro dilemma.

3. Bertrand Russell, *Human Society in Ethics and Politics* (New York: Simon & Schuster, Inc., 1962), p. 38.

4. All biblical passages quoted are from the King James Version unless otherwise noted. Although this is a poor translation in many ways, it is considered by many Christians to be the *only* version in English which is the word of god, so it is used here. However, other translations have been consulted, and no comment regarding the bible hinges on the use of a particular translation. Where other translations are quoted, it is only for clarity.

5. Jesus apparently did not know the ten commandments very well. In Mark 10:19 he lists "defraud not" as a commandment. Of course, it is not one of the ten.

6. Instead of *"bring judgment on themselves,"* the King James Version has *"shall receive to themselves damnation."*

7. How curious that the bible says that Moses was the meekest of all men (Num. 12:3)!

8. Thomas Paine, *The Age of Reason* (Amherst, N.Y.: Prometheus Books, 1996), p. 20.

9. Some Christians attempt to exonerate Jesus from the charge of lying in this case by insisting that, back in those days, paradise was in hell! Of course, there remains a conflict between Matthew 12:40, in which Jesus says that he will spend three days and three nights "in the heart of the earth," suggesting a downward direction, while such people as Elijah (2 Kings 2:11) and Enoch (Heb. 11:5) were taken *up* to god long before the time of Jesus.

10. Only the version found in Exodus 34 is specifically identified as "the ten commandments" in the bible. That version bears little resemblance to the first set of commandments, from Deuteronomy 5 and Exodus 20, which are usually called "the ten commandments." According to the bible, god incorrectly declares in Exodus 34:1 that the second set of commandments is identical to the set that Moses broke. However, the Exodus 34 set does not forbid murder, lying or theft. The Exodus 34 set *does* forbid boiling a kid (goat) in its mother's milk, it insists on the observance of the feast of weeks, it requires the observance of the feast of unleavened bread, it mandates giving all the firstborn sons to god, and so on. It is this set of commandments, in fact, which was placed in the famed ark (Deut. 10:1–5). Christians who advocate observing the ten commandments usually don't realize the serious contradiction regarding which set of ten commands are supposed to be the correct ones.

11. Darrel Henschell, *Perfect Mirror? The Question of Bible Perfection* (Fayetteville, Ariz.: Hairy Tickle Press, 1996), p. 65.

12. Immanuel Kant, *Groundwork of the Metaphysic of Morals*, James W. Ellington, trans. (Indianapolis, Ind.: Hackett Publishing Co., 1981).

13. Ibid., p. 421 on the traditional pagination.

14. Immanuel Kant, *Religion within the Limits of Reason Alone*,

T. M. Greene and H. H. Hudson, trans. (New York: Harper & Row, 1960), p. 3.

15. Ibid., p. 4.

16. John Stuart Mill, *Utilitarianism,* reprinted in *Ethical Theories: A Book of Readings,* A. I. Melden, ed. (Englewood Cliffs, N.J.: Prentice Hall, Inc., 1967), p. 395.

17. Ibid., p. 395.

18. Ibid., p. 399.

19. Edith Hamilton, *The Greek Way* (New York: W. W. Norton & Company, Inc., 1964), p. 184.

20. Aristotle, *The Nicomachean Ethics,* David Ross, trans. (New York: Oxford University Press, 1980), section 1006b36.

20. Ibid., Book II, section 1.

21. Paul Kurtz, *Forbidden Fruit: The Ethics of Humanism* (Amherst, N.Y.: Prometheus Books, 1988), chapter 3.

Question #3

How Can Atheists Have a Purpose to Their Lives?

The belief that atheists cannot have a purpose to their lives is widespread. This belief is vague, usually not well thought out, and often unsupported by any reasons. It is also false. I usually try to address this issue with two main points. As was the case regarding ethics, if it can be shown that theism lacks a particular feature, then the theistic charge that atheism does not have this component is less of a problem for the atheist. Atheism cannot be condemned as strongly for the absence of some element if those making the charge do not have it either. Furthermore, if the atheistic view can be shown to possess this desirable feature while theism does not, then atheism would have been shown to have a clear advantage over this rival view. I will address each part of this two-stage approach in a separate section. First, I will show that theism has not been shown to be an adequate basis for providing a "purpose" to life; and, second, there are good reasons to believe that one's life can be filled with purpose without belief in god.

A. It is unlikely that theism can provide life with a purpose.

Although it is not clear what the Christians and other theists mean by "purpose," and different believers probably mean different things by the term, there are good reasons to believe that theism, specifically Christianity, cannot serve as an adequate system for providing life with a purpose.

1. The more morality and the purposeful life are linked, the more Christianity cannot provide life with a purpose.

Many people are inclined to believe that morality is an integral part of the purposeful life. If it is, then it can be said that theism cannot provide a sufficient basis for a "purpose" to life because, as explained above, theism cannot serve as a basis for morality.

2. Predestination robs life of purpose.

Versions of Christianity which promote predestination, the view that one is condemned to hell or saved even before one is born, are particularly liable to the charge that theism cannot provide life with a purpose. What would be the purpose to life if one's moral status, one's eternal reward or punishment, had already been decided even before one was born?

Predestination implies that there is no free will, that we cannot choose what we will or will not do. If humans cannot make choices or decisions, if we are little more than robots whose moral worth is already decided even before we are born, then it is not clear how the Christian could show that such a life could be filled with purpose. No theologian has ever been able to satisfactorily explain this.

To the extent that free will is a necessary element in a life of purpose, the doctrine of predestination makes a purposeful life impossible.

3. The doctrine of original sin conflicts with the life of purpose.

Versions of Christianity which promote the doctrine of original sin, the view that all people are condemned to eternal torture for the sin of Adam, are susceptible to the charge that they cannot provide a purpose to their life.

Many Christians promote the view that human beings are basically evil. For some Christians, the view that they are morally vile is central to their worldview. On this topic Robert Ingersoll, the nineteenth-century jurist, orator, and freethinker wrote:

> The ministers are in duty bound to denounce all intellectual pride, and show that we are never quite so dear to God as when we admit that we are poor, corrupt and idiotic worms; that we never should have been born; that we ought to be damned without the least delay. . . . The old creed is still taught. They still insist that God is infinitely wise, powerful and good, and that all men are totally depraved. They insist that the best man god ever made, deserved to be damned the moment he was finished.[1]

Should the purpose of one's life be founded on the notion that he or she is vile and despicable? How can one aspire to be noble and great if one's most fundamental belief about humanity is that we can never be anything other than worthless, offensive, and disgusting?

If self-worth is related to a life of purpose, the Christian doctrine of original sin undermines the possibility of a life with purpose.

4. The doctrine of salvation by grace conflicts with the life of purpose.

Many Christians who adhere to the doctrine of original sin also believe in salvation by grace. On this view, one is not saved by one's merit, but by god's fiat or arbitrary decision. One can never perform any act or set of acts which would change the fact that one deserved eternal torture. Unfortunately, since this makes everyone equal with regard to merit, god's decision about who gets saved becomes, by definition, arbitrary.

However, if you are saved only by god's arbitrary decision, by "grace," and not by anything you have done to deserve salvation, there is no point in being moral. Others see to it that you are saved or damned, and you have no say in the matter. As far as morals are concerned, what would be the point of any particular action as opposed to any other? If you are condemned to hell because of the sin of someone else, and there is nothing you can ever do to change the fact that you deserve eternal damnation, morality becomes pointless. You could never deserve worse than damnation, and nothing you could do could ever make you deserve any better, so why be moral on this Christian view? Why do anything? What is the purpose here? If human beings cannot become better than they are, it is not clear how life could be anything other than a meaningless farce in which each person is powerless to shape his or her life and moral worth.

5. Performing god's will is not acceptable as a purpose to life.

Many Christians often claim that serving god is the purpose to life, that doing god's will, at any cost, is the only thing that can make life worth living. There are good reasons to believe that this is false.

a. Slavery is not a sufficient purpose to life.

Can total submission make life worthwhile? Can slavery be ennobling? Mindless obedience is praiseworthy in dogs and horses, but in humans it is repulsive, especially if it is to a being who orders genocide and other horrible acts, as commanded by the god of the bible. Do we admire the unswerving obedience of Hitler's best generals? Should we sing songs about history's most faithful butchers? Obedience in itself is no virtue.

Some theists claim that humans must obey god because god is the creator. This principle seems false. Humans beings are created by their parents, but no one these days thinks that the purpose of children is to be slaves to their parents, although many societies at one time have held such views for young children. Parents who order their children to steal or kill are thought unfit to be parents, so it does not seem to be true that creators have a right to make slaves of their creations. Sometimes Christians will respond that parents are not the ultimate creators of their children, and it is only the creator of everything which has a right to make slaves of everyone it creates. This is an assertion which needs to be sup-

71

ported, but there is no reason to believe that this principle is true. Until there is some reason to believe that the principle is true, it remains a dubious claim at best.

An interesting thought experiment can provide a reason for believing that the principle of obeying the creator is false. Suppose that the Christian god appeared tomorrow and confessed that he is really an evil demon—but he is still the creator. This being, the creator, proceeds to order Christians to slaughter innocent children, rape young girls, enslave people of certain races, and engage in other such social practices as the god of the Old Testament orders. The creator being states that these actions are intended to cause misery and suffering. No good is supposed to result from them at any time in the future. Would the Christian still feel morally compelled to obey this being simply because he is the creator? A negative answer here shows that the principle that "one must obey the creator because he is the creator" is false. A positive answer—that the Christian would obey anyone, even an evil demon, simply because he is the creator—shows a lack of moral values. The latter type of person does not care who the master is as long as he or she can be a slave. Such a view is morally repugnant.

b. God's will cannot be determined.

Of course, even if it were the case that one ought to do what god wills in order to lead a life of purpose, since it cannot be determined what god's will is, the claim that one ought to obey god is worthless. The bible provides vague, inadequate, immoral, and contradictory principles. People as unlike as Hitler, Mother Teresa, Mohandas K. Gandhi, Heinrich Kramer, and James Sprenger have claimed to be fulfilling god's will with their activities. The last two are the authors of the infamous *Malleus Maleficarum* (Witches' Hammer), the handbook widely used at the end of the fifteenth century both to discover and to punish witches. The book describes methods of torturing and killing suspected witches with red-hot irons, suspending them by their thumbs, burning them at the stake, pouring boiling water on them, and other supposedly divinely ordained methods of justice and investigation.[2] (Is there any atrocity which has *not* been performed in the name of god?)

As we saw in the case of ethics, if so many different activities and goals can be "justified" as being god's will, and there is no reliable method for distinguishing acting according to god's will and *mistakenly thinking* that one is acting according to god's will, then the claim to be acting according to god's will becomes meaningless. Anyone from a serial killer to a priest can claim to be fulfilling god's will, and there is no test which the theist can use which would falsify the claim of one and not the other.

Theists wildly disagree about the will of god. Christians disagree about the permissibility of abortion, the morality of euthanasia, the equality of women, the doctrine of predestination, original sin, the inerrancy of the bible, the existence of hell, and other fundamental issues. Christians cannot give a uniform response regarding the will of god on *any* of these issues, and, of course, they also disagree with other religions who also claim to be acting according to god's will. Since determining the will of god with any degree of certainty is impossible, if fulfilling the will of god were the purpose in life, then leading a life of purpose would be impossible.

c. The theist cannot show that there is a god.

In addition, to the extent that god's existence itself cannot be shown (a matter to be addressed later), the claim that one ought to perform god's will is weakened. If it cannot even be shown that there is a god, claims about god's will ring hollow.

6. The claim that a god, and only a god, could give a purpose to one's life is untenable.

On the theistic view, it is never sufficiently explained how a being such as a god can give meaning and purpose to life. Most theistic writers simply assume that beings such as gods can do this, but the relationship between a god and the purpose to life is usually not addressed.

a. The purpose to life could not be simply that we ought to stay out of hell.

Some theistic writers hold that god gives a purpose to life because if we do not perform god's will, then we will be damned to hell. That is hardly a purpose, and perhaps it is worse than not having one. Imagine a sadist who enjoys putting young children in irons, who visits them every day in the dungeon, and who feeds them and keeps them off the rack in exchange for praise. It would be accurate to state both that the incarcerator is not worthy of praise and that the prisoners could not be said to be leading meaningful lives, if that were all there was to their lives. The same observations would be appropriate to the situation if it were the case (as it is not, fortunately) that there is a god who threatens to torture those who do not worship him. Bullying and torture may be effective means of coercion, but being on the receiving end of such abuse is not having a purpose to life, and the sadistic person dispensing the punishment deserves to be denounced, not praised.

In any case, history has clear cases of those who have led a life filled with purpose but who met a gruesome end in the fight for their cause, which shows that avoiding pain or punishment for oneself is not always what makes life worthwhile. Imagine the case of a fellow who would be willing to go to hell forever if it meant that a friend would be spared the agony of the damned. Such self-sacrifice and love for another are exactly the sorts of qualities which would be said to *give* noble purpose to life. Someone who would be willing to do that for a friend would be considered a good, admirable person. Thus, if going to hell is compatible with having a life of purpose, and with being a good person, then staying *out* of hell cannot be the purpose to life.[3]

b. It is false that only a being as wise as god could give purpose to life.

Sometimes theists assert that only god could imbue life with purpose because only god is wise enough to do so. It is not clear what this is supposed to mean, but on any reasonable interpretation this view is easily shown to be either false or nonsensical, so it may be rejected.

(i) All the conflicting varieties of Christianity, as well as other religions, boast that their views can provide a purpose in life. However, their claims regarding god are contradictory. Some religions hold that there is one god, some say that there are more than one, and so on. It is not possible for all of these claims to be true, so it is known that at least some, if not all, of them are false. Thus, even if it were the case that we could not determine which of the world's religions are false, it *can* be determined that in many cases people can seemingly live a life of purpose even when their god does not exist. Perhaps it would be more accurate to say that believers of religions whose god or gods do not exist do not appear to lead lives any less meaningful than those of Christians, whose god has yet to be shown to exist. Christians would say that the ancient Greek gods did not exist, yet many pious Greeks led lives indistinguishable in purpose from those of modern Christians. Thus, since, as the Christians would say, those gods never existed, it is clearly false that gods are required to lead a life at least as purposeful as that of a Christian.

(ii) On the other hand, if the claim is that only god knows the secret purpose to life, then the claim is nonsense. It reduces to a claim indistinguishable from simply asserting that life has no purpose at all. What sense does it make to state that there is a purpose which no one knows? Whether there is a secret purpose or no purpose, in each case the effect for human life is the same—no known purpose. Theists who assert that god is required for life to have meaning and then deny that the meaning is known render pointless whatever supposed meaning life may have, since, in such a case, human beings must give their lives meaning whether god exists or not, since the meaning to life is unknown. So why bother to insist that god must exist in order for life to have a purpose?

(iii) In some cases theists claim that only god, in his omniscience, knows what is best for each person, so only god knows what you should do, what your particular purpose should be. However, because god's will cannot be determined, this claim, too, is indistinguishable from that of having a secret purpose or no purpose at all, so the claim is both unsupported and pointless.

Summary of section A:

1. The more morality and a purposeful life are linked, the more Christianity cannot provide life with a purpose.
2. Predestination robs life of purpose.
3. The doctrine of original sin conflicts with the life of purpose.
4. The doctrine of salvation by grace conflicts with the life of purpose.

5. Performing god's will is not acceptable as a purpose in life.
6. The claim that a god, and only a god, could give a purpose to one's life is untenable.

Therefore, it is unlikely that theism can provide life with a purpose.

If my thesis for section A is correct, the atheist is no worse off than the theist on the issue of the meaning of life. Any case for a purpose to life on the atheistic view would show that the atheist is in a better position than the theist in this respect. This advantage will be shown in section B.

B. There are good reasons to believe that life can have a purpose without belief in gods.

There are many ways in which one can have a purpose in life without requiring belief in deities. In addition, the lives of many atheists certainly give every indication that they are filled with purpose.

1. Atheists can explain how one's life can have purpose without belief in gods.

What does it mean to have a purpose in life? Is a purpose essential for happiness, or is it required only to make one's life significant instead of meaningless, with no guarantee that happiness may result? Detailed answers to these questions are beyond the scope of this work, since, even if it were the case (which it is not) that life could have no meaning without gods, the fact that life would be unfulfilling would not be sufficient reason to believe that gods exist. Whether or not there are gods is an issue that should be decided on the basis of its truth, not on the basis of whether it is pleasant or useful to believe in gods. However, a basic outline of how one may answer these questions may not be out of place here. In addition, the reader must be reminded here that, as noted earlier, it is not the case that all atheists agree to a certain set of core beliefs. Thus, it must be understood that the following remarks are not representative of the beliefs of all atheists.

a. The question "What is the meaning of life?" is often misleading.

First, it should be noted that many nonphilosophers tend to assume that the question at hand should be asked in the form: "What is the purpose to life?" or the age-old "What is the meaning of life?" However, these questions are too vague to be of much use. They are loaded with unwarranted assumptions. For example, the question "What is the meaning of life?" is most often asked in a manner which, unfortunately, assumes all of the following: life can have a meaning, each person's life can have a meaning, each person's life can have only one meaning, all people's lives have the same meaning, each person's life already has a meaning, no one's life can lose its meaning, no one has to do anything to get a meaning to life, and so on. All of these assumptions, *because* they are assumed and not the product of investigation into the relationship between purpose and life, tend to hinder those who are interested in the real issue, which is exploring the possibility of leading

78

a life that has meaning or purpose, and, if it is possible to lead such a life, how one should go about doing so.

What should be asked first are questions such as the following: What is it to have a purpose to life? Is it possible for someone to have a life filled with purpose? If I don't already have a purpose to my life, can I get one? Philosophers throughout history have answered these basic questions in different ways.

b. Philosophers have explained how one's life can have a purpose without belief in gods.

There is no mystery about the fact that life can have a meaning, a purpose, without gods. For our brief outline, let us define a purpose to life as that part of life which productively shapes the course of one's life and the selection of goals according to certain criteria. The life of purpose is guided by goals which can inspire one to the improvement of both oneself and the world. The life of purpose is also one in which the agent, the one whose life it is, finds fulfilling employment of his or her talents in pursuit of these goals.

(i) The life of purpose includes improvement of both oneself and the world.

Developing one's talents, constantly challenging oneself to become a better person, is considered by many to be an important part of the life of purpose. Developing one's talents can take many forms. Developing the moral virtues, learning more about the nature of the world, working constantly to improve one's relationships with others are all part of what it is to improve oneself. Different people will interpret the notion of self-improvement in different ways, but clearly such a project enables one to deal better with adversity, and it is a rewarding task in itself. When life becomes difficult,

79

when one's goals have been frustrated, it is comforting to be able to look back upon what one has accomplished, or at least tried to accomplish. A pianist who struggles to master a particularly difficult piece may fail but he is still made greater by the attempt.

The use of one's talents to improve the lot of others is also part of the life of purpose. The artist who creates works that deepen our understanding of some aspect of life, the agronomist who makes it a little easier to feed the hungry, the teacher who expands the minds of students—all use their abilities to make the world better than it would be otherwise. The value of such effort is to be found in the opportunity to use one's talents creatively, in the appreciation from those whose lives have been touched, and in the advantage of living in a world that is constantly being made more agreeable for human life. Although not all occupations have positive results as visible as those of the artist or scientist, the aspect of creative, positive contribution can be found in any activity— except those of criminals, where the employment usually makes the world a worse, not better, environment.

(ii) The life of purpose includes the utilization of one's talents.

It should be obvious to anyone that an important part of having a life filled with purpose is accomplishing something, preferably many things. The use of one's talents, whatever they may be, in the quest toward improvement of oneself and the world is the best way to lead a satisfying life.

An accomplished logician once told me that the secret to happiness is to find something you liked doing and then find some way to get paid doing it. Obviously, this is something of an exaggeration, but the basic idea is sound. If what one loves doing is part of the project of improving oneself or the quality of human life, then it is the perfect occupation. This fellow loved doing logic. He did it as his profession, and he did it in his spare time. He was engaged in an activity, the study of logic and arguments, which was complex and challenging enough to occupy his talents for the rest of his life. I have never met a happier person.

Having a zeal for a particular activity when that activity fills the need for the project of improvement makes for a fulfilling life. On this topic Bertrand Russell noted:

> The forms of zest are innumerable. Sherlock Holmes, it may be remembered, picked up a hat which he happened to find lying in the street. After looking at it for a moment he remarked that its owner had come down in the world as the result of drink and that his wife was no longer so fond of him as she used to be. Life could never be boring to a man to whom casual objects offered such a wealth of interest. Think of the different things that may be noticed in the course of a country walk. One man may be interested in the birds, another in the vegetation, another in the geology, another in the agriculture, and so on. Any one of these things is interesting if it interests you, and, other things being equal, the man who is interested in any one of them is better adapted to the world than the man who is not interested.[4]

The person who is constantly striving to become more than what he or she is at present will have a broad range of interests and, consequently, will be presented with more opportunities in which to employ his or her talents. This utilization of one's talents, this use of one's abilities in a productive and satisfying way, is an important part of the life of meaning. One does not get a purposeful life, *one creates it.* To the extent that one is willing to put forth the effort to make positive changes in oneself and the world, one is rewarded with a life filled with purpose.

In *Exuberance: A Philosophy of Happiness,* Paul Kurtz emphasizes the creative aspect of human activity in his prescription for happiness:

> As I see it, creative achievement is the very heart of the human enterprise. . . . The destiny of man, of all men and of each man, is that he is condemned to invent what he will be—condemned if he is fearful but blessed if he welcomes the great adventure. We are responsible in the last analysis, not simply for what we are, but for what we will *become*; and that is a source of either high excitement or distress.[5]

The creation of meaning for one's existence is a positive and empowering aspect of life. Why might someone feel distress at the thought of having to do something to make one's life have meaning? Many theists prefer to think that one can lead an important, purposeful life without doing much in the way of self-improvement, and this belief, perhaps, is part of the explanation of why theism is so popular. One can, on most versions of theism, expend no effort to develop oneself and yet supposedly feel that one is of tremendous cosmic importance because, apparently, one merits the attention of an omnipotent being, even if the attention is for the purpose of damnation. The theist's do-nothing approach to the life of purpose is just a gimmick. It is the easy approach to life, but one gets out of life what one puts into it. One who does nothing becomes nothing. The easy road through life is not the best road, but the easy road sells bibles and gets donations. It promises something for nothing. All you need to do to have a purposeful life is to hold certain beliefs—that there is a god, that Jesus died for your sins, and so on. How much effort does that take? The only effort needed is the mental energy to suppress one's critical thinking skills so that belief in the absurd ideas of theism may be maintained. But *caveat emptor*—let the buyer beware. If someone promises something for nothing, it is usually too good to be true. In the case of theism, it is neither good nor true.

It is true that some theists do not believe that one must simply hold certain beliefs in order for life to have a purpose. Some Christians feel that activities such as feeding the hungry, providing disaster relief, guiding delinquent teenagers, and similar endeavors are what provide meaning to life. However, any other beliefs or activities which the theist may add to the requirements for a life of purpose can be believed or pursued by the atheist, so the theist has no advantage with regard to purpose in life when mere belief in gods is not at issue. In other words, atheists and agnostics can *and do* perform those same activities, so the theist who states that it is those altruistic actions which provide life with purpose must concede that the atheist can have a purpose to life also. Further, since nontheists perform acts of kindness and charity, it is false that only belief in god could inspire a person to perform such acts, which is another claim popular among theists.

The atheist does not promise something for nothing. It takes effort, determination, self-confidence, and sometimes a little ingenuity to constantly strive to improve oneself and the world. Not everyone is willing to try to create a meaningful life, especially since there are no guarantees. What can be promised is that the beliefs that give one's life purpose and meaning will not be unintelligible. There will be no evasive language, no appeals to mysterious forces, no squelching of native curiosity, no insistence that you are not supposed to know. Every principle, every explanation, will be open to view, and examination, even attack, is invited. That's how it should be, after all. Life is too important to waste; it is a precious commodity that should be used carefully, not profligately. It should not be dedicated to ideals without regard to their nature and their truth. The purpose of life, the value of human existence, should not be a secret. It is easily located in the realm of human action and interaction. Kurtz writes:

Human life has no meaning independent of itself. There is no cosmic force or deity to give it meaning or significance. There is no ultimate destiny for man. Such a belief is an illusion of human-kind's infancy. The meaning of life is what we choose to give it. Meaning grows out of human purposes alone. Nature provides us with an infinite range of opportunities, but it is only our vision and our action that select and realize those that we desire. . . . Thus the good life is achieved, invented, fashioned in an active life of enter-prise and endeavor. But whether or not an individual chooses to enter into the arena depends upon him alone. Those who do can find it energizing, exhilarating, full of triumph and satisfaction. In spite of failures, setbacks, suffering, and pain, life can be fun.[6]

The meaning of life is to be found in accomplishment, and this is cause for celebration.

Theists tend to mistakenly believe that the lives of atheists are depressing or emotionally barren. While this may be true of some atheists, it is not true of any I have met. It is true, however, of many Christians I know. Life without belief in god can be productive and emotionally satisfying. Bertrand Russell's three-volume autobiog-raphy begins with a prologue entitled "What I Have Lived For." In it, he explains:

Three passions, simple but overwhelmingly strong, have gov-erned my life: the longing for love, the search for knowledge, and unbearable pity for the suffering of mankind. . . . This has been my life. I have found it worth living, and would gladly live it again if the chance were offered me.[7]

The theist has nothing to fear regarding the purposeful quality of life when belief in gods is gone. On the contrary, as Sigmund Freud said, "When a man is freed of religion, he has a better chance to live a normal and wholesome life."

2. The lives of many atheists have been filled with purpose.

Many atheists have led lives which give every indication that they are filled with purpose.

Bertrand Russell (1872–1970), Nobel prize-winning philosopher, who was tremendously influential in the field of analytic philosophy, was jailed for his pacifist beliefs during World War I. He was also active in the nuclear disarmament movement during the sixties, and he championed many social causes. A social critic, he wrote hundreds of articles and dozens of books. Russell, who died at the age of ninety-seven, lived a full, rewarding life. Any theist who would deny that a life such as that of Bertrand Russell was one of purpose must support this claim, and no theist has ever been able to do this.

Scottish philosopher David Hume (1711–1776) was not a theist. James Boswell, a devout Christian, visited Hume on his deathbed. Although Boswell thought Hume was a good and decent man, he was still disturbed that Hume could feel so much satisfaction about his own life, even in the face of death. Hume is considered one of the most influential philosophers of all time. His *Enquiry Concerning Human Understanding* is still influential today. In many ways, Hume's work changed the way in which philosophers interpreted important philosophical issues.[8]

Margaret Sanger (1883–1966) was a tireless, dedicated crusader for women's right to birth-control information. Though she began her fight in 1914, it was not until 1936 that birth-control information became legally available. Often in trouble with the law and narrow-minded public officials, Sanger struggled against tremendous legal, religious, and public opposition to her work. The masthead of her newsletter on birth control read: "No gods, no masters." Surely Sanger led a life of purpose.

Sigmund Freud (1856–1939), the founder of psychoanalysis, led a life of purpose and dedication to his work. Freud's work was revolutionary in shaping the way in which we now understand human motives and the human condition.

Influential horticulturist Luther Burbank (1849–1928) bred a wide variety of fruits, vegetables, and flowers. He called himself an infidel—an unbeliever—yet his life was filled with creative and influential works.

Other atheists whose names are often recognized include: science-fiction writers like Ursula K. LeGuin, Isaac Asimov, Harlan Ellison, Piers Anthony, and Arthur C. Clarke; actors Marlon Brando, Sir John Gielgud, John Larroquette, and Peter Ustinov; comedians George Carlin and Paula Poundstone; linguist and social commentator Noam Chomsky; magicians Penn Jillette and Teller; composer and musician Randy Newman; science-fiction author and screenwriter Michael J. Straczynski; novelists Gore Vidal and Kurt Vonnegut Jr.; and the philosophers A. J. Ayer, Paul Churchland, Patricia Churchland, Daniel Dennett, Theodore M. Drange, Paul Edwards, Anthony Flew, Sidney Hook, J. L. Mackie, Michael Martin, Kai Nielsen, Sir Karl Popper, and W. V. O. Quine. And many more.

The list of atheists on the broad definition, the definition which includes agnostics, would include thousands of other famous people throughout the history of human civilization. Theravada Buddhism practitioners, found mainly in Sri Lanka and Southeast Asia, are, if not atheists, at most indifferent to the existence of gods. They believe that salvation is achieved by the individual; gods are of no help in this process. Some practitioners of Hinduism, such as those who follow the Sankhya or the Nyaya system, are atheists. Jainism, which developed from Hinduism in the sixth century B.C.E., is also considered atheistic and currently numbers its followers at about four million.[9] If such people, and *many* others, could lead full, influential, satisfying, and creative lives in the absence of belief in god, then the Christian must either admit that life can have a purpose without belief in god or explain how it may be that lives which certainly seem to be filled with purpose are, in fact, not so. Atheists have yet to encounter a good argument for the latter.

A comprehensive philosophy of life which includes atheism as one of its features is often called humanism. Humanism is founded on the use of reason and science; in its contemporary version it promotes both individual and social responsibility. There are a number of different kinds of humanism which explain how life can have a purpose without gods.

Most atheists become humanists as they create meaning for their lives and expand their horizons. Because this book is concerned with atheism, not humanism, the reader is referred to the list of suggested readings for further details about humanism.

Conclusion

A. It is unlikely that theism can provide life with a purpose.
B. There are good reasons to believe that one's life can have a purpose without belief in god.
  1. Atheists can explain how one's life can have purpose without belief in god.
  2. The lives of many atheists have been filled with purpose.

Therefore, the charge that atheists cannot have a purpose to their lives is groundless.

Many Christian apologists attempt to refute atheism by explaining at length how meaningless life would be if human beings did not have eternal life, how tragic it would be if relationships ended at death, how unjust the world would be if the righteous were not rewarded and the wicked punished in the hereafter, and other supposedly undesirable states of affairs. This is supposed to show that we should believe in god. Such an approach may be characterized as an argument from wishful thinking, which has the following general form:

The Wishful Thinking Argument:

1. If god does not exist, then some undesirable consequences would follow.
2. One should not believe that certain undesirable consequences will follow.

---

3. Therefore, one should not believe that god does not exist.

Of course, a clever apologist will take two hundred pages or more to say this; otherwise, he or she would appear to be advocating something rather silly. Obviously, god does not exist because it would be inconvenient or undesirable if he did not, yet many a book purporting to refute atheism is little more than an elaborate restatement of the wishful thinking argument. As Saul Bellow noted: "A great deal of intelligence can be invested in ignorance when the need for illusion is deep."

It should be obvious that the wishful thinking argument is invalid, since it can be parodied quite easily to show that this line of reasoning leads to false conclusions. Suppose that someone who is accused of embezzlement is in court, on the verge of losing the case, and the only thing that can prevent this disaster is the serendipitous discovery of a large amount of money within the next five minutes. There are no legends, reports, or witnesses to the existence of any nearby treasure, but the person in need of money, having read a sufficient number of works on apologetics, proposes the following solution to the legal dilemma:

The Spontaneous Resources Argument:

1. If a leprechaun does not hand me a large sum of money within the next five minutes, then some undesirable consequences would follow.
2. One should not believe that certain undesirable consequences will follow.

---

3. Therefore, one should not believe that a leprechaun will not hand me a large sum of money within the next five minutes.

Similarly, a window washer who has just fallen from the top of a skyscraper could feel relief, comfortable in the knowledge that, on similar reasoning, since falling to his or her death would be undesirable, a parachute will appear on his or her back just in time to be put to good use. Obviously, arguments of this form are absurd, but they continue to play an influential role in the minds of many theists.

Some theists have asked me whether I am afraid of death. They reason that, if there is no god, death is the end of one's existence. It would be terrible if that were so, and thus we must believe that god exists. But they may just as well have asked me whether I am afraid of cockroaches. In either case the existence of god is irrelevant. Either god exists or he does not, but whether I would be afraid of death or not, or whether I would like or dislike the situation if god did not exist, has nothing to do with the truth of the matter. Is it *true* that god exists? This is an entirely different question from whether I would *like* for god to exist. God will no more begin to exist if I fear death than a can of insecticide will appear in my cupboard if I am afraid of cockroaches.

If there is no god, and life is not as some people wish it to be, that's just something each person will have to face. Fortunately, however, life does *not* become empty, unbearable, hopeless, or morbid because god does not exist. There is extensive humanist literature on the subjects of life, love, death, and other issues, literature that makes a solid case for the purposeful, and amply rewarding, nature of human existence in the absence of gods. There is no need for wishful thinking.

Notes

1. Robert G. Ingersoll, *Some Mistakes of Moses,* reprinted in Stein, pp. 148–49.

2. Heinrich Kramer and James Sprenger, *The Malleus Maleficarum,* Rev. Montague Summers, trans. (New York: Dover Publications, Inc., 1971).

3. Christians may be tempted to mention here, for some reason, that Jesus was willing to die and go to hell for me. To this I need simply point out that, according to the story, Jesus was rid of these inconveniences in less than three days. Apologists who reply that Jesus spent an eternity in hell in three days, and I have met some who do, are using words bereft of meaning. They hardly merit a response, since they have not given any intelligible statement to refute. In any case, maybe their anticipated eternity in heaven will only last three days, too.

4. Bertrand Russell, *The Conquest of Happiness* (New York: Liveright Publishing Corp., 1955), p. 95.

5. Paul Kurtz, *Exuberance: A Philosophy of Happiness* (Amherst, N.Y.: Prometheus Books, 1977), p. 172.

6. Ibid., p. 174.

7. Bertrand Russell, *The Autobiography of Bertrand Russell*, vol. 1 (Boston: Little, Brown and Company, 1967), p. 4.

8. It is not clear whether Hume was an agnostic or, as narrowly defined, an atheist. It is clear, however, that he thought that the meaning of life was not dependent upon belief in, or the existence of, gods.

9. Jains take several vows in their religion, one of which is that of *ahimsa*, or noninjury to life. To keep this vow, Jain monks will strain their water before drinking it to avoid accidentally ingesting aquatic insects, sweep the path in front of them with a broom as they walk to avoid stepping on minute bugs, and wear a mask over their mouths to prevent inhaling flying insects. If the Christian wishes to maintain that devotion to religious principles is what gives meaning to life, then these Jain atheists undoubtedly have lives filled with purpose. In fact, their degree of devotion shames that of the average Christian.

Question #4

Doesn't the Bible Show
That God Exists?

Christians often try to use the bible to show that god exists. To this there are at least two responses: (A) arguments that the bible is evidence for god's existence fail, and (B) there is good evidence that the bible is unreliable. Both (A) and (B) show that arguments for god's existence which rely on the bible are worthless. On the basis of (A) *alone* arguments for god's existence which rely on the bible may be disregarded, but the fact that the bible is unreliable is so little known among Christians that evidence of the bible's unreliability will also be presented.

A. Arguments that use the bible as evidence of god's existence fail.

Although it is a common practice to use the bible as a tool to seemingly demonstrate the existence of god, there are conclusive objections to this approach.

1. Arguments that assert that the bible is the word of god are circular.

A class of arguments which I have encountered all too often in connection with the bible are those having the following form:

1. The bible is the word of god.
2. The word of god is free of error.
3. The bible says that god exists.

---

4. Therefore, god exists.

Arguments such as this are hopelessly flawed. Obviously, to show the truth of the first premise, that the bible is the word of god, one would first have to show that there is a god in order to show that the bible is the word of that god. In other words, one would have to prove the truth of the conclusion in order to prove the truth of one of the premises. This type of reasoning is defined as circular, and such arguments can never demonstrate the truth of their conclusions because the conclusion is *in* the argument's premises.

2. Arguments for god's existence based on biblical prophecy fail.

Christians sometimes present noncircular arguments for god's existence based on prophecies found in the bible. These arguments are unsuccessful.

a. Arguments that rely on biblical prophecy have a common form.

Arguments for god's existence which depend on bible prophecy take a form similar to the following general outline:

1. The bible contains a prophecy regarding such-and-such an event.
2. The event prophesied came to pass.
3. There is no alternative explanation for this prophecy coming true other than that the Christian god exists and gave this information to his prophet so-and-so.

---

4. Therefore, the Christian god exists.

The event and prophet in question varies according to which supposed prophecy is being used. Arguments of this form are extremely popular among Christian apologists.

b. There are conclusive objections to arguments based on biblical prophecy.

Despite their popularity, arguments based on biblical prophecy can easily be shown to fail.

(i) There are alternative explanations for prophecy.

Although not circular, the argument from bible prophecy can be dismissed. Even if the bible did contain a prophecy of an event which later came to pass, this would not prove the existence of god. There are always alternative explanations for prophecy which do not involve gods.

For example, a race of extraterrestrials could have told someone, in a technologically advanced manner, a manner which would seem miraculous, that a certain event would happen. Then these beings could have brought about that event, again using advanced technology. The clever alien scenario shows that the hypothesis that a god exists is not the only possible explanation for the fulfillment of prophesies. In order to conclude that a god must have been responsible for a supposed instance of prophecy, all other possible explanations must first be ruled out as impossible or as far less likely than the god hypothesis. Given the extraordinarily strong claim about the nature of the theistic god, however, it would seem that almost any other explanation would be more likely than that of theism. Time-traveling human beings, amazing coincidences, carefully planned hoaxes, all would be more likely explanations for the supposed fulfillment of a prophecy than the god hypothesis because these claims are weaker than the theistic claim. The nontheistic claims are less extraordinary and thus more likely to be true, so it is unlikely that the theist could ever eliminate these other possible explanations. Premise (3) of the biblical prophecy argument cannot be shown to be true and the argument fails. (More will be said of extraordinary claims in chapter 7, section A.)

(ii) The argument from biblical prophecy does not show that the Christian god exists.

Even if it were granted that a prophecy and its subsequent prophesied event took place, and it is granted for the sake of argument that this was due to the intervention of a god, this would not show the existence of any particular god. Many gods in human mythology are said to be capable of bestowing the gift of prophecy. Other traditions have their prophets. Will the Christian grant that these cases of prophecy are genuine? If not, why should anyone grant that they took place in the Christian case? And if the Christian does grant that someone in another religion was able to make an accurate prophecy because of the Christian god, then an adherent of that religion could say the same of Christianity and claim that the Christian prophets were able to prophesy because of the non-Christian god. A Hindu god, for example, could have been responsible for informing supposed Christian prophets about the future. The Christian who asks, "Why would the Hindu god do that?" can be met with the response that the particular Hindu god in question works in mysterious ways.

All that is needed to undermine the argument from prophecy is the possibility that some other god may have been responsible for the supposed prophecies of the bible. It seems unlikely that the Christian can rule out this possibility, and this would undermine premise (3). Thus, the argument does not work.

(iii) It cannot be shown that there are *any* genuine cases of successful biblical prophecy.

Despite the fact that some apologetic books would have you believe that the bible contains hundreds of fulfilled prophecies, *it cannot be shown that any one of them is a genuine case of fulfilled prophecy.*

Some criteria are needed in order to distinguish cases of lucky guesses from those of true prophecy. Let us define a genuine prophecy as one that satisfies the following five criteria.

1. The prophecy must be clear, and it must contain sufficient detail to make its fulfillment by a wide variety of possible events unlikely.

For example, a prophecy that "something bad will happen tomorrow" is too vague. So many unfortunate events happen in the world every day that this prophecy could easily be made and fulfilled without its explanation requiring appeal to divine influence. The same can be said of such prophecies as "One of your relatives will receive bad news next week," "A mayor will be involved in scandal," and "A black thing will appear in the sky and scare many."

2. The event that can fulfill the prophecy must be unusual or unique.

A prophecy regarding the make of vehicle, type of clothing, age, name, and other details of the person who delivers the newspaper to one's house every morning would not qualify as a genuine prophecy. Common events cannot be the subject of prophecy, since they occur with such regularity that no divine power is required to anticipate further instances of them. An exception would be applicable in cases where a class of events, or its participants, are unknown to the prophet at the time of the prophecy, but it later became common. For example, a prophecy made today about a particular secretary using a computer keyboard in an a certain law office would not qualify as genuine because such events are now common, but if the prophecy had been made several hundred years ago, that would be another matter.

97

3. The prophecy must be known to have been made *before* the event that is supposed to be its fulfillment.

This criterion is obvious. Anyone can prophesy after the fact.

4. The event foretold must not be of the sort that could be the result of an educated guess.

If two nations amass their troops along a common border and begin exchanging mortar fire every few days, a prophecy that the two countries will be engaged in full-scale war within six months would prove nothing. Many people could predict that without divine intervention.

5. The event that fulfills the prophecy cannot be staged, or the relevant circumstances manipulated, by those aware of the prophecy in such a way as to intentionally cause the prophecy to be fulfilled.

For example, suppose that someone discovers the following prophecy: "a rabbit will squeal in pain at three o'clock in the afternoon at the site of the Battle of Palmito Ranch on September 24, 2000." The person could then take a bunny there to give it a good slap at the appropriate place and time, but this would prove nothing. No divine influence would have been needed for these circumstances to occur.

These do not seem to be unreasonable criteria for prophecy. Unfortunately for the Christian, *not a single case of supposed bible prophecy can satisfy the criteria.* In some cases the evidence that the prophecy fails is in the bible itself.

Because it is known that most of the books of the Old Testament were written centuries after the death of the person for whom the book is named, and the report of the prophecy *and* of its ful-fillment were thus written long after each of those supposed events, most of the prophecies of the Old Testament fail to satisfy criterion (3). The same is true of most of the New Testament prophecies; the gospels were written decades after the events they supposedly describe. Since the prophecy and the description of its fulfillment were written at the same time, it cannot be shown that the prophecy preceded the described event.

Other prophecies are shown to be false by other kinds of evi-dence in the bible. For example, 2 Kings 22:20 states the prophecy that King Josiah would die in peace, that he would *"be gathered unto thy grave in peace."* However, 2 Kings 23:29–30 and 2 Chronicles 35:23–24 tell us that Josiah died because he was shot full of arrows and then transported on a chariot.

Many people are impressed with the prophecy in Jeremiah 31:4, which states that *"Again I will build thee, and thou shalt be built, O virgin of Israel."* This is taken to mean that the state of Israel will come into being sometime in the future, which happened in 1948. However, this prophecy stated no specific time when this would be fulfilled. Does it take divine inspiration to state that at some unspec-ified point in the future people will come together and found a state? It is not clear that this is so much a prophecy as an expression of hope. In any case, it is a moot point, since Amos 5:1–2 states: *"O house of Israel. The virgin of Israel is fallen; she shall no more rise."* No divine inspiration is needed to prophesy that Israel either will or will not rise. I can say the same of any nation or city. When one utters a prophecy of event A, and the negation of A, e.g., "Israel will rise or not rise," one of these is guaranteed to come true. But one is guaranteed to be false as well. So much for this prophecy.

One of the most popular prophecies from the bible is that pre-dicting the destruction of the coastal city of Tyre. Ezekiel 26:3–36 explains at length that Nebuchadnezzar will lay siege to Tyre and destroy it, that he will take its money and goods, that the city will "be built no more" and "be no more," and that the city will be covered with water; speaking to the city, the bible says *"though thou be sought for, yet thou shalt never be found again."* The most mysterious thing about the Tyre prophecy, however, which, perhaps, defies rational explanation, is that it is often showcased in Christian apologetics as an example of a fulfilled prophecy, since *it is well known that this prophecy did not come true.* Any history book about the period will explain that Nebuchadnezzar's thirteen-year siege was unsuccessful, and the bible admits as much in Ezekiel 28:18, where it is explained that Nebuchadnezzar had no loot to show for all his trouble. The city was later conquered by Alexander the Great, but it was rebuilt and is currently inhabited. Strangely, some apologetics books about bible prophecy even contain a photograph of Tyre, as if to say "here is the city of which the prophecy was fulfilled that it would never be found again." There is an airport near Tyre, and any travel agent would be glad to book a flight there. Proof that the prophecy failed is just a phone call away.

Many New Testament prophecies can be shown to have failed as well. In fact, many of them that are said to have been fulfilled were never prophesied at all. Many a Christian has repeated thousands of times that Jesus rose on the third day "in fulfillment of the scriptures," but one may search the Old Testament in vain for any such prophecy about rising on the third day. It is not there.

Regarding his resurrection, Jesus supposedly stated *"so shall the Son of man be three days and three nights in the heart of the earth"* (Matt. 12:40). Compare Matthew 17:23, 27:62; Mark 8:31, 9:31; Luke 24:46; and 1 Cor. 15:4, which insist on at least three days. If Jesus were correct about his own schedule, three days *and* three nights contain a total of seventy-two hours, and he would have to remain dead for that period of time. Yet the bible account says otherwise. Jesus was said to have been crucified, died, and been buried on a Friday afternoon. Mark 15:26 says Jesus was crucified at the third hour, at nine o'clock, but John 19:14 has Jesus still at his trial at noon. In any event, Jesus was reportedly crucified on Friday. The gospels agree that he rose on Sunday morning, the first day of the week (Matt. 28:1, Mark 16:2, Luke 24:1, and John 20:1). That's not three days and three nights. Even if Jesus had been dead and buried by one o'clock in the afternoon on Friday, which is unlikely, given the text of John, if he rose by six in the morning on Sunday, that's forty-one hours, which is more than a full day short of the seventy-two hours he prophesied.

Christians who insist on counting the partial Friday and the sliver of Sunday as full days may get Jesus his three prophesied days, but no such calendar juggling will be able to squeeze three nights out of this brief time, so Matthew 12:40 is a failed prophecy.

There is no prophecy in the Old Testament regarding a third-day resurrection for Jesus to fulfill, and Jesus did not fulfill his own prophecy about being dead for three days and three nights.

Many Christians are also familiar with Matthew 2:23: *"And he came and dwelt in a city called Nazareth: that it might be fulfilled which was spoken by the prophets, He shall be called a Nazarene."* The gospel of Matthew routinely uses "spoken by the prophets" to refer to Old Testament scripture, but there is no such prophecy in the Old Testament. In fact, the term "Nazarene" and "Nazareth" do not appear in the Old Testament at all. The prophecy fails to satisfy criterion (3), and perhaps the rest of the criteria as well, since the prophecy cannot be found.

Isaiah 7:14 is often taken to prophesy the virgin birth of Jesus: *"Therefore the Lord himself shall give you a sign; Behold, a virgin shall conceive, and bear a son, and shall call his name Immanuel."* However, scholars are well aware that the term translated here as "virgin," the Hebrew word *'almah*, is best translated as "young woman," who may or may not be a virgin. The Hebrew word

101

bethulah means "virgin," but that is not the word used in the Isaiah verse. Some modern bibles, such as the Revised Standard Version, use the correct translation of this passage and do not use the word "virgin." Furthermore, the Hebrew text is in the present tense; the verse states that a young woman *is* pregnant, not that she will become so. Further, anyone who takes the trouble to read the verse in context will see that the event in question was not a prophecy about some event in the distant future. It was intended to be a sign to King Ahaz of Judah, the king who asked Isaiah for help. The birth of the son was supposed to be a sign to the king that an attack by a hostile alliance, including Israel, would be unsuccessful against Judah. Isaiah also admits, in 8:3–4, that he "went unto the prophetess" just to make sure that she was pregnant. The verses in 7:15–16 make it clear that the sign was supposed to be of events in Isaiah's day, since these state that the alliance would fail before the child was old enough to know good from evil. Clearly, none of this has any relation to Jesus or Christianity. As a prophecy about Jesus, it is none, so it fails to satisfy all of our criteria. The prophecy also failed in Isaiah's time, since it failed to satisfy several criteria, not the least of which is that the attack on Judah was successful after all (2 Chron. 28:1–5).

There are many New Testament passages which prophesy that Jesus would return soon. Matthew 16:28 has Jesus say, *"Verily I say unto you, there will be some standing here, which shall not taste of death, till they see the Son of man coming in his kingdom."* Luke 9:27 has a similar verse: *"But I tell you of a truth, there be some standing here, which shall not taste of death, till they see the kingdom of God."* This turned out to be not a truth, but a lie, since Jesus has not returned, and those who were standing there being addressed, if there ever were such an event, are long dead. In Matthew 10:23, Jesus tells his followers that if they are persecuted in a city, they should flee to another city, and that *"Ye shall not have gone over the cities of Israel, till the Son of man be come."* Of course, Israel was never so large that it would take over two thousand years to cross it on foot and visit all its cities, so another one of Jesus' own prophecies fails. There are many passages which refer to the time shortly after the death of Jesus as "the last days," "the end," "the end of the world," and other phrases which indicate a quick second coming.[1] Jesus' own supposed prophecy about himself fails, as do these other predictions about the Second Coming.

One by one, the prophecies of the bible have been exhaustively examined by scholars and theologians. Not one can be shown to be a case of a genuine prophecy which has been fulfilled. Tim Callahan's book *Bible Prophecy: Failure or Fulfillment?* is recommended for those who have doubts about the utter failure of biblical prophecy.

B. There is strong evidence that the bible is unreliable.

Bible scholars are of two kinds: the biased and the unbiased. The difference can be seen in the way in which they treat the sacred texts of other religions. If he uses the same methods of analysis on the bible that he uses on other books, that is a good sign that the scholar is unbiased. The best unbiased bible scholars hold that there are good reasons to believe that the books of the bible are *un*reliable sources. Accuracy and historical reliability are major problems for the books of the bible, even for the New Testament. These scholars are agreed on a number of facts about the bible.[2] Here are just a few of the more interesting facts.

1. Almost all of the books of the bible are anonymous.

With the exception of a few of Paul's letters in the New Testament, no one knows who wrote the various books of the bible. As far as the gospels are concerned, it is not known whether any one of them was originally written by a single author or a committee. It is known that all of them have been edited and altered in various ways. The gospels weren't given the names of authors until the second century, and this was done according to mere rumors and hearsay.

2. The gospels were written decades after the events they purport to record.

Those who wrote the New Testament were *not* eyewitnesses to Jesus' life or resurrection. It is known that the gospels were written long after the supposed life of Jesus. They are anonymous accounts based on hearsay by anonymous people.

3. We do not have any original documents of any of the books of the bible.

All we have are copies of copies of copies, we don't know how many times removed from the originals. Most of the complete gospels we have are fourth-century documents.

4. The entire New Testament was originally written in Greek.

If Jesus did exist, his words were undoubtedly in Aramaic, not Greek. No one knows who translated his words (if there were any), or whether the translator(s) was (were) competent.

5. At some points in the Church's history, lying to promote its cause was not only not discouraged, but encouraged.

The New Testament manuscripts we have were kept and copied by an institution, the early Church, which is *known* to have forged documents and to have altered existing manuscripts in order to promote its cause. *This alone raises serious concerns about the reliability of the gospels.*

6. Ancient documents critical of Christianity were sought out and destroyed.

It is no secret that the early Church did not tolerate criticism of its views. Many early writings which attacked Christian claims or practices were burned. For example, Porphyry of Tyre, an early critic familiar with Christian theology and scripture, wrote a number of books criticizing Christianity, including *Kata Christianon* (*Against the Christians*), which was ordered burned in 448 C.E. In Porphyry's *Against the Christians: The Literary Remains,* R. Joseph Hoffmann writes, "Not only were Porphyry's books destroyed, but many of the works of Christian writers incorporating sections of Porphyry's polemic were burned in order to eliminate what one critic, the bishop Apollinarius, called 'the poison of his thought.' "[3] Thus, it is difficult to make an informed decision about many Christian claims because they have seen to it that it is impossible to get a balanced viewpoint. The clergy have ensured that all that remains are biased, altered copies of anonymous manuscripts.

7. Some manuscripts are different from other copies of the same book.

The old manuscripts of the New Testament which we do have contain conflicting passages within copies of the same book. By some estimates, 10 to 20 percent of the New Testament manuscripts we have *disagree, sometimes on points fundamental to Christianity.*

For example, the last twelve verses of the gospel of Mark, Mark 16:9–20, are *known* to have been added much later than the time the rest of the gospel of Mark was written. These verses do not appear in any of the early copies of this gospel. These forged verses contain the only post-resurrection appearances of Jesus in Mark. Since Mark is thought to be the earliest gospel, it is interesting that the earliest supposed biography of Jesus' life contains no report of any eyewitnesses who saw Jesus after the resurrection.

Another example is 1 John 5:7 (*"There are three who bear record in heaven, the Father, the Word and the Holy Spirit; and these three are one."*). This verse did not appear in 1 John until the *fourteenth century!* It is missing from all early Greek manuscripts and from the fifth-century Latin Vulgate translation. The world's top bible scholars have for years been unanimous in declaring that this passage is a later insertion and does not belong in the bible, *yet this verse is the one most often cited to try to show that the doctrine of the trinity has biblical support!* This forged verse in 1 John 5:7 is still found in the "authorized" King James version, which dates to 1611, and some other translations.

The insertion of forged verses is most often detected only when scholars discover an older copy of the same book which does not have the verse in question. There is no way to tell how many other forged verses there may be which have not been detected. Remember, all we have are copies of copies of copies, and at any point in the copying process someone could easily have added or deleted a verse or two. In some cases there are *thousands* of variant readings among the manuscripts of the same book of the bible. Since there is no original manuscript, in many cases we have no idea which version is closest to the original.

8. Most of the books of the New Testament are known to be forgeries.

It was an accepted practice in many schools of the ancient world to write works in the style of some revered teacher or well-known person. Those who were most adept at forgery were praised. This class of literature, called *pseudepigrapha*, was done in the name of famous people, both historical and legendary, from Plato to Adam, from Isaac to Aristotle. It was not considered immoral to write such works, and many manuscripts which originated in this way have later been mistakenly thought to be genuine. Most of the books of the New Testament are known to be forged works of this sort.

Scholars now know that half of the letters said to be by Paul, and all the letters of James, Jude, and John could not have been written by the persons whose names are associated with them. In fact, the two letters said to be by Peter not only could not have been written by Peter, *they are probably not even by the same author!* Of course, the gospels themselves may be thought of as forgeries if you consider as a forgery any anonymous book that is later attributed to someone who did *not* write that book.

9. The gospels are not independent accounts of the life of Jesus.

Many Christians think that it is not a problem that the gospels differ in many details because the gospels are, so the Christians say, four independent accounts written many years after the events they

107

describe. Don't different people often describe the same events in different ways? We would expect them to differ, wouldn't we?

Unfortunately, that is not the way the gospels were written. For example, Matthew, Mark, and Luke are not independent accounts at all. Scholars agree that there is a literary relationship among them; that is, some parts of them are rewritten, more detailed versions of one of the other gospels, and, some scholars think, perhaps based on another document, called "Q," which is now lost. In other words, major portions of the first three gospels were revisions; they were rewrites with interpolations (new, forged material). Figuring out which parts were based on which others is an issue well known to scholars as "The Synoptic Problem." Thus, rather than having, as many Christians think, four independent accounts of Jesus' life, there may be only one or two original accounts. Exactly which parts are interpolations and which are original is not certain. What is certain is that major portions of the gospels were plagiarized from other material.

10. The development of the bible undermines its reliability.

One may wonder who decided which books to include in the bible and how they did it. Most Christians are completely ignorant of the process which led to the canonization, the official church recognition, of the books that are in the standard King James bible.

In the time Jesus is supposed to have lived, it had not even been established which books should be included in the *Old* Testament. To complicate matters, in the first two centuries C.E. (Common Era), there were *dozens* of literary gospels, acts, letters and apocalypses in circulation. Only some of these were later accepted as canonical and included in the bible. Some of the books which did not make it include those attributed to Mary Magdalene, Thomas, Paul, Andrew, Bartholomew, Judas Iscariot, Pontius

Pilate, and many others. Some of these gospels described Jesus' years as an infant, his descent into hell, and other adventures.

Historians tell us that one of the first attempts to canonize the currently accepted twenty-seven books of the New Testament was the Festal letter by Athanasius of Alexandria in the year 367 C.E. His influence was such that many people agreed with him in time. By 405 C.E. the pope agreed with Athanasius, and one canonization was, for the most part, settled. However, many Christian sects did not, and still do not, accept that canonization.

But how was this official adoption of books, the canonization, decided? Scholarship was rudimentary in those days. People did not have access to information in the way we do now. Although in some cases a book was rightly declared a forgery (sometimes someone exposed the forger!), for the most part nothing was known of the origin of a given book or even how a particular church in a certain region had come to possess it. In most cases they could not check sources, facts, or any such information relevant to the question of authenticity. Some groups decided on a canon of books by a vote. Is that a reliable way to decide whether a given work is authentic? Shouldn't scholarship decide the issue? It is not known whether those who voted for the authenticity of a particular book did so based on religious, personal, political, or other grounds. What is known with certainty now is that they were incorrect. As noted above, almost all of the books of the New Testament are *known* forgeries.

In "The History of the Text and Canon of the New Testament to Jerome," noted scholar C. S. C. Williams states that "the early history of the growth of the Canon of the New Testament is lost in obscurity."[4] Most early Church writers favored quoting from books which are *not* accepted now as canonical rather than citing those which are. Those who wrote, selected, copied, and edited the earliest Christian writings are unknown.

Other facts about the canonization process hardly inspire confidence. For example, some books, such as Hebrews, were hotly disputed throughout the fourth century and beyond. The Church father Tertullian, around 200 C.E., thought that Barnabas had written it. A few decades later Church leader Origen considered *Hebrews* anonymous. The Muratorian Canon, based on a Greek canon of 180–200 C.E., does not include Hebrews. Some thought that it was written by Clement, a Church leader who flourished around 200 C.E.; others thought that Clement at least knew the identity of the real author. Early in his career, St. Augustine (354–430 C.E.) accepted Hebrews as Paul's, but later he changed his mind and considered it anonymous.

With appropriate sarcasm, Voltaire (1694–1778) lists some of the "reasons" which church leaders have given as to why, with the abundance of available gospels, there are only four gospels included in the standard canon:

> At length, four Gospels are chosen; and the great reason for having that number, as stated by St. Irenaeus, is, that there are only four cardinal points; that god is seated on cherubims [the second-class, winged angels who support the throne of god], and that cherubims have four different shapes. St. Jerome, in his preface to Mark's Gospel, adds to the four winds and the four-shaped animals, the four rings of the poles, on which the box called the ark was carried.
>
> Theophilus, of Antioch, proves that as Lazarus was dead only four days, we can consequently admit only four Gospels; St. Cyprian proves the same thing by the four rivers that watered paradise. We must be very impious not to yield to such reasons as these.[5]

Surely readers need not be informed that such "arguments" for the acceptance of only four gospels are nonsense. One may just as easily "prove" that there should be three gospels because of the trinity; twelve because of the number of disciples; forty because of the number of days (or nights) that Jesus is said to have spent in the desert, as well as the number of days that Jesus is said to have spent with his disciples after the resurrection (Acts 1:3);[6] one hundred fifty-three, for the number of fish Simon Peter hauled up in his net after Jesus was resurrected; or one because of the number of heads cut off of John the Baptist. Is this any way to determine the authenticity of manuscripts? Of course not.

The case of the unreliability of the Old Testament is even worse news for the believer. *The Oxford Companion to the Bible* states: "No traditions have survived concerning the authorities who fixed the canon of Hebrew scriptures, or about the internal order of the books, or about the underlying principles that determined their sequence."[7]

All of the Old Testament books are anonymous. Although the first five books of the bible, commonly called the Pentateuch, are often attributed to Moses, it is known that he could not possibly have written them. This evidence is in the bible itself. Those books include an account of Moses' death and burial, and they mention cities and regions not named until centuries after the death of Moses, and other matters. For similar reasons, scholars know that Samuel did not write the books of Samuel, Solomon did not write the Song of Solomon, and so on. All Old Testament books show signs of editing, revision, and interpolation of new material. Some, such as the book of Jeremiah, are a jumbled hodgepodge of repetitive, unrelated, or incomprehensible chapters and verses.

Today the Roman Catholic Church accepts seventy-three books as their bible: the thirty-nine books of the Old Testament, the twenty-seven of the New Testament, and books such as Tobit, Judith, Bel and the Dragon, and others that are considered deuterocanonical, also called apocryphal. The latter types of works, of which there is a wide variety, are books which had enough polit-

111

ical or theological support for their authenticity that they could not be rejected outright, but not enough that they could be accepted into the canon proper. At one time all the King James Versions of 1611 had the Apocrypha sandwiched between the Old and New Testaments. The Greek Orthodox Church accepts even more works in their bible, including 1 Esdras, the Prayer of Manasseh, Psalm 151, and 3 Maccabees. The Eastern Orthodox churches have the thirty-nine Old Testament books, the twenty-seven New Testament, and ten deuterocanonical, for a total of seventy-six. The Ethiopic church has a total of eighty-one books, although they divide some books of the Old Testament differently.

Are all of these Christian bibles the word of god? Are all the books contained in them inspired? Why should one use one of the bibles with a certain number of books and not others? Clearly the origin of the bible, and the lack of authentication of the books before they were accepted, undermines the reliability of the bible.

11. Biblical accounts contradict facts about nature and the ancient world.

Many books of the bible abound in factual error. The term "factual error" is used here to distinguish this type of error from a contradiction. A factual error is considered a mistake because it conflicts with known facts. A contradiction is considered an error because it conflicts with another biblical passage, and it is *impossible* for both passages to be true.

(i) The Old Testament contains page after page of error.

The Old Testament contains inaccurate historical assertions. For example, the eighth chapter of Joshua reports that Joshua conquered the ancient city of Ai, yet archaeological evidence, according to *Biblical Archaeology Review*, "has wiped out the historical credibility of the conquest of Ai as reported in Joshua 7–8."[8] Daniel 5:30–31 has Darius the Median ascending the throne of Babylon when Belshazzar was killed, but historians know that it was Cyrus the Great who conquered the throne in 539 B.C.E., and there is no record of any Darius. Scholars agree that he is a fictional character, probably invented to try to salvage the failed prophesies in Isaiah 13:17, 21:2 and Jeremiah 51:11 that a Median would conquer Babylon. The book of Daniel was written in the second century B.C.E., which about three centuries after the events it purports to describe. This may explain its many historical errors. Regarding the conquest of Canaan found in Joshua and Judges, historian William H. Stiebing Jr. writes, "It is only in recent times, through the development of biblical criticism and archaeological research, that we have come to realize that the Conquest narratives are not historical.[9] The evidence against the historical accuracy of the Old Testament is overwhelming. Of course, the myths of Adam and Eve, Noah's ark and such are allegorical at best. No historian or bible scholar would even consider defending these tales as historical accounts. The Old Testament contains many errors concerning biology and nature. Leviticus 11:6 and Deuteronomy 14:7 state that hares chew the cud, and Leviticus 13:19 and Deuteronomy 14:11–18 tell us that bats are birds. The bible also tells us that insects have four legs (Lev. 11:23).[10] Genesis 30:37–42 describes how one can produce spotted and striped cattle by having them mate near some striped and speckled sticks.

The report that the sun stopped in the sky so that god's representatives would not be forced to stop the butcher of enemies (Josh. 10:12–14) clearly shows that biblical reports cannot be taken at face value. Such an event would have been visible worldwide, but the text of Joshua is the only report of it. The earth's rotation stopped for a day, but no other nation on earth seems to have

113

noticed! 2 Kings 20:11 has a related event. It is not clear which is the more astonishing: the cessation of the earth's rotation or that anyone in the modern age still believes that this occurred. This absurd text from Joshua, as well as Ecclesiastes 1:5 and Psalms 19:4–6, 93:1, and 104:5, are largely responsible for the condemnation of Copernicus' heliocentric theory in 1616, and Galileo's defense of it in 1633.[11]

The bible even contains mathematical errors. Ezra 2:3–64 gives a census of a congregation of people, with the total given is 42,360, but anyone who reads the verses and does the addition will have to confess that the tally is really only 29,818, for a difference of 12,542. The book of Nehemiah, 7:8–66, also gives a census, and the total given is 42,360. The total is really 31,089, for an error of 11,271. Of these computational errors Thomas Paine remarked, "What certainty, then, can there be in the bible for anything?" and "These writers may do well enough for Biblemakers, but not for anything where truth and exactness is necessary."[12]

(ii) The New Testament, too, is factually unreliable.

The New Testament tells us in Matthew 2:16 that Herod, king of Judea at that time, ordered killed all the male children in the region of Bethlehem who were two years old or younger. Ancient historians, both those who later chronicled Herod's abuses of power and those who lived in Judea when this was supposed to have occurred, say nothing of such a massacre, and they would certainly have called attention to such an event! The incident is not even mentioned anywhere else in the bible.

Matthew 27:45 explains that there was darkness "over all the land" when Jesus died. No contemporary records of eclipses or similar phenomena support such a claim. Matthew 27:52–53 states that when Jesus died the graves of many of the saints opened, and when Jesus

114

rose the saints rose also and went into town and were seen by many people. Historians such as Philo-Judaeus, who lived in Jerusalem at the time, know nothing about Jesus or any other resurrections. What historian would have failed to mention a crowd of dead saints come to life? Such a singular event would have been deemed one of the most amazing miracles in the history of humanity, yet not even the other gospel writers had the nerve to relate this obvious fiction.

The books of the bible are implausible accounts. There are *many* other historical mistakes in the bible, far too many to cover here. If the bible cannot be trusted to be accurate about mundane historical events, the natural world, or mere sums, why should anyone trust it when it makes wild, completely unsubstantiated claims about ghosts, miracles, angels, and other supernatural occurrences?

12. The bible contains many contradictions.

In addition to contradicting facts, the bible also contradicts itself. Citing some of the hundreds of biblical contradictions would be, in itself, uninteresting. However, a number of the contradictions are relevant to some of the basic claims of Christianity. Below are a few examples.

a. Does god repent?

One would think that the issue of whether god repents would be an important element of the conception of god. If god repents, or changes his mind, this would imply that god is not omniscient, that god makes mistakes.

Genesis 6:6, 18:20–32, Exodus 32:14, Numbers 14:20, 1 Samuel 15:35, 2 Samuel 24:16, and Jeremiah 18:8 show that god changes his mind. Numbers 23:19–20, 1 Samuel 15:29, and other passages hold that god does not.

Exodus 33:2–3 has god explain that he can't even trust himself! God is afraid that he will do something he will regret later—destroy the Israelites in a fit of anger. Even if there were a god, if god can't trust himself, why should anyone else trust him?

b. Does god punish children for the sins of their parents?

Deuteronomy 24:16 and Ezekiel 18:19–20 state that offspring should not be punished for the sins of their parents. However, Exodus 20:5, 34:7, Numbers 14:18, Deuteronomy 5:9, Isaiah 14:21–22, and other verses state that god does indeed punish children for the actions of their parents. Deuteronomy 23:2 describes a law that punishes one who is born out of wedlock and also punishes that person's offspring for *ten* generations.

c. Is anyone righteous?

Romans 3:10–12 states that "There is none righteous, no, not one. . . ." Many Christians seem to relish in the accusation that everyone is detestable. However, the bible states clearly that at least some people have been righteous, such as Noah (Gen. 7:1), Job (Job 1:1, 1:8, 2:3), and Zechariah and his wife Elizabeth (Luke 1:6). The bible suggests that some who pray are righteous (James 5:16), and 1 John 3:6–9 holds that Christians become righteous.

d. Are we justified by faith or by works?

The bible is explicit that *"a man is not justified by the works of the law, but by the faith of Jesus Christ . . . not by the works of the law: for by the works of the law shall no flesh be justified"* (Gal. 2:16). This is also stated in Romans 3:20 and 28 (*"a man is justified by faith without the deeds of the law"*), and in Ephesians 2:8–9. How-

116

ever, James 2:17 and 2:24 state just as clearly that faith alone is "dead" and *"Ye see then how that by works a man is justified, and not by faith only."* Compare also Romans 2:13 that *"the doers of the law shall be justified."* Matthew 7:21 states that *"only he who does the will of my Father who is in heaven"* (NIV) will enter the kingdom of heaven, not those who simply call on Jesus.

e. Does god keep his promises?

Deuteronomy 7:9 and Titus 1:2 are two passages which state that god is honest and keeps his promises. Christians hope so, since they rely on god keeping promises for their salvation. Unfortunately, there are passages in the bible which show that god cannot be trusted to keep a promise.

God promised that David was to have a kingdom forever (2 Sam. 7:11–16 and 2 Kings 8:19), that David would always have one of his descendants on the throne (Jer. 33:17–21), that this promise was unconditional, and that it was *not* dependent upon anyone keeping god's law (Ps. 89:29–37). Elsewhere in the bible, it is stated that god's promise *is* conditional (1 Kings 9:3–5), and David's rule was destroyed in the reign of Zedekiah (Jer. 52:12–14).

Genesis 17:8 states that god promised to give the land of Canaan to Abraham. But Abraham never received the promised land (Gen. 25:8, Acts 7:5, Heb. 11:13). God promised the same land to Moses (Exod. 6:8), yet Moses did not receive the land either (Num. 14:30–34, 32:10–13).

Jeremiah 18:8 has god explain that if he has stated that he will destroy a nation and that nation turns from their evil, then god will *"repent of the evil that I thought to do unto them."* However, after King Josiah of Judah was warned that god was angry at him and his nation, he and his people swore to keep god's covenant (2 Kings 23:3). They got rid of the idolatrous priests (2 Kings 23:5), de-

117

stroyed or defiled places of worship of other gods (2 Kings 23:8–15), and held the Passover better than anyone (2 Kings 23:21–22). The bible says that never before or since has there been any king who *"turned to the LORD with all his heart, and with all his soul, and with all his might, according to all the law of Moses"* (2 Kings 23:25). 2 Chronicles 34:33 tells us that Josiah had all his subjects swear loyalty to god, and that the people followed god without fail. Despite all this, and despite the promise explained in Jeremiah, god still decided to destroy Judah anyway because of the things Josiah's grandfather had done. Thus, god violated his promise that he would not destroy a nation which turned away from evil. Recall, too, that, according to Deuteronomy 24:16 and Ezekiel 18:19–20, children should not suffer for the sins of their parents.

f. Are all things possible if one has faith?

Matthew 17:20, Mark 9:23, and Luke 17:6 state that anything is possible if one has faith, even faith like that of a mustard seed (which they erroneously thought was the smallest seed). In other words, even the smallest possible amount of faith is enough to allow one to command a tree to go plant itself in the sea, and it would obey.

Yet both Matthew and Mark also record instances where Jesus himself was unable to perform "mighty works" because of the unbelief of those around him (Matt. 13:58, Mark 6:5). In Mark 8:22–25 Jesus has to make two attempts to heal a blind man because the first attempt was inadequate. Are we to believe that Jesus, who is supposed to be god incarnate, who created the heavens and the earth, could not heal a blind man in one attempt? If all things are possible for one who has faith, why couldn't Jesus heal the blind man in one try? Did Jesus not even have faith as small as a mustard seed, the smallest possible amount of faith? If Jesus did not have faith why should anyone else?

g. Will all who call on Jesus' name be saved?

Romans 10:13 (quoting Joel 2:32): *"For whosoever shall call upon the name of the Lord shall be saved."* But Matthew 7:21 has Jesus state: *"Not every one that saith unto me, Lord, Lord, shall enter the kingdom of heaven; but he that doeth the will of my Father which is in heaven."*

h. Will god always be there in times of need?

Psalm 145:18 states that *"The LORD is nigh unto all them that call upon him, to all that call upon him in truth."* Hebrews 13:5, quoting Joshua 1:5, states that god has said *"I will never leave thee, nor forsake thee."*

Of course, Jesus' last words, according to two of the gospels, were *"My god, my god, why hast thou forsaken me?"* (Matt. 27:46, Mark 15:34). Psalm 10:1 suggests that god sometimes hides in times of trouble.

i. Was Jesus god?

John 10:30 has Jesus state *"I and my Father are one."* Passages supporting Jesus' identity as god also include Colossians 2:9, John 20:28, John 14:9, and Titus 2:13.

However, there are many other passages which make it clear that Jesus and god are not the same. John 14:28 has Jesus state that *"my Father is greater than I."* Something can't be the same as another thing and also be greater than it. Other passages which show that Jesus was not god include Luke 18:19, Matthew 19:17, Mark 13:32, Mark 14:36, John 5:20, and Acts 2:22–24. Matthew 12:31–32 shows that blaspheming against Jesus is not as terrible as blaspheming against the Holy Spirit, so obviously they cannot be identical either. John 8:42 has Jesus state, *"I came from God and*

119

now I am here. I have not come on my own; but he has sent me" (NIV). If Jesus is sent *by* god, he can't *be* god, especially if he admits that he did not send himself, that he did not come on his own.

John 20:17 has Jesus say, *"I ascend unto my Father, and your Father; and to my God, and your God."* Apparently Jesus has the same god as his disciples. If Jesus *is* god, why would he pray to someone else? Why would Jesus pray, as in Mark 14:35, if *"in him dwelleth all the fullness of the Godhead bodily"* (Col. 2:9)? To whom was he praying? Jesus' last words (from Matt. 27:46 and Mark 15:34), stating that he had been forsaken by god, also show quite clearly that he could not be god. One cannot forsake or abandon oneself.

Clearly, the bible contradicts itself on these and *many* other issues central to Christianity. The bible is so contradictory that it cannot be used to form a coherent core of beliefs for Christianity. To construct a consistent set of beliefs from the bible, believers *must* reject many parts of the bible.

Christians who have a more enlightened view of the bible, who accept the judgment of the world's scholars with regard to the origins of the books of the bible and the mythical roots of the fables about Jesus, often object to attacks on the bible by arguing that only some portions of the bible are to be believed. They state that parts of the bible are metaphorical, other parts are poetry, other stories are simply attempts to relate some religious experience, and that one is not supposed to understand the bible so literally. The bible is still a worthwhile read, they suggest, because it is inspirational though not necessarily divine or even true.

One reply to this objection of a "liberal" interpretation of the bible is that no nonarbitrary interpretation of the bible allows some parts of the bible to be rejected and other important parts to be preserved. In other words, on what basis may one reject the resurrection of an entire crowd of saints (Matt. 27:52–53) and yet maintain that Jesus was resurrected? It is not clear that there could be any criteria which would eliminate the former and not the latter. Once it is admitted that significant reports in the bible are false, once legitimate scholarly techniques are used to eliminate portions of the previously sacred text, then the other myths of the bible will succumb just as easily to the light of reason.

One who decides to believe some fabulous stories from the bible and not others must have a preconceived notion of what result is desired. One is, in effect, making god in his or her own image. The stories and claims which support the person's idea of god are believed, and those which are in conflict with that view are rejected. Yet many theologians and schools of thought have taken this approach, and they have created a wide variety of differing ideas of god, from that of a cruel tyrant to that of a loving father figure. This would seem to show that this process can tell us much about the character of the person doing the selecting and rejecting of verses, but, since there is no nonarbitrary way to show that one interpretation is correct and another false, it can show nothing about the nature or existence of any god.

Many contemporary bible scholars and theologians are willing to abandon any or all of the miracle claims of the bible and accept the book simply as inspirational in that it challenges human beings to aspire to be moral and compassionate. This view is problematic, however, in that the bible is filled with deplorable moral values. It is also written in such a way as to lend itself to a reading which takes its stories to be fact, not fiction. If the liberal scholar will always be plagued by those who misunderstand the biblical accounts as history instead of myth, why not find more appropriate fictional material? Even Aesop's fables, or something like them, would be more suitable. Although both the tales of Aesop and the bible have stories about talking animals, I have yet to meet someone who thought that the animals of Aesop really existed and talked. However, I have met people who have told me that they believe that the serpent and the ass of the bible actually talked. In any case, another advantage which Aesop's fables have over those of the bible is that those of Aesop contain far less carnage and sadism, if any, and are thus much less objectionable as moral lessons for children.

Another problem with the view of the bible as inspiring myth instead of fact is that it remains a relevant objection that there is no way to determine whether any given scholar's interpretation of a metaphor is correct. Every generation of Christians has claimed to have the correct interpretation of the bible, and each subsequent generation has been just as certain of yet another reinterpretation of the book. In any case, if belief in gods and miracles is no longer required for the bible to be of value, on this liberal interpretation, then the atheist has little quarrel with these scholars except with regard to the poor selection of fables.

Summary of section B

Because these and other facts about the bible show it to be an unreliable document, it *certainly* cannot be considered strong evidence for the existence of god. The bible seems to be so unreliable that it could hardly be considered evidence at all. To the extent that the holy books of other religions suffer from the same class of problems, they, too, cannot be considered evidence for the existence of their respective gods.

Conclusion

A. Arguments using the bible as evidence of god's existence fail.
 1. Arguments that assert that the bible is the word of god are circular.
 2. Arguments for god's existence based on biblical prophecy fail.
B. There is strong evidence that the bible is unreliable.

Therefore, arguments for the existence of god which rely on the bible may be dismissed.

Christians who cry "Foul!" and protest that the verses of the bible used above were distorted in meaning because they are taken out of context are invited to take their own bible, look up these verses, and read as much of the context as they please. The contradictions, absurdities, and errors of all kinds, which have been known for centuries, will remain, and there are many others just as damaging. C. Dennis McKinsey's *The Encyclopedia of Biblical Errancy* and Darrel Henschell's *The Perfect Mirror? The Question of Bible Perfection* are good starting points for further investigation.

Notes

1. A few such verses are the following: Acts 2:17; 1 Corinthians 7:29; Philippians 4:5; 1 Thessalonians 4:15; Hebrews 1:2, 9:26, and 10:37; James 5:8; 1 Peter 1:20 and 4:7; 1 John 2:18; and Revelation 1:1, 1:3, 3:11, and 22:10.

2. Cf. R. Joseph Hoffman, "The Origins of Christianity" in *On the Barricades: Religions and Free Inquiry in Conflict,* Robert Basil, Mary Beth Gehrman, and Tim Madigan, eds. (Amherst, N.Y.: Prometheus Books, 1989), pp. 233–44.

3. R. Joseph Hoffmann, *Porphyry's Against the Christians: The Literary Remains* (Amherst, N.Y.: Prometheus Books, 1994), pp. 164–65.

4. C. S. C. Williams, "The History of the Text and Canon of the New Testament to Jerome," *The Cambridge History of the Bible,* G. W. H. Lampe, ed. (New York: Cambridge University Press, 1969), 2: 42. Williams's article provides most of the information used in the remainder of the paragraph.

5. Voltaire, "The Important Examination of the Holy Scriptures," R. Carlile, trans. (London, 1819), reprinted in Stein, p. 166.

6. Other, contradictory, passages suggest that Jesus was on earth for much less time. The gospels of Mark and Luke indicate that Jesus left that same day he was resurrected. John suggests that it was at least eight days after the resurrection. Acts 1:3, of course, holds that it was forty days. That the resurrection and post-resurrection stories in the gospels are hopelessly contradictory has been known for centuries.

7. *The Oxford Companion to the Bible,* Metzger and Coogan, eds. (New York: Oxford University Press, 1993), p. 98.

8. See "Joseph A. Callaway: 1920–1988," *Biblical Archaeology Review,* November/December 1988, p. 24.

9. William H. Stiebing Jr., *Out of the Desert?: Archaeology and the Exodus/Conquest Narratives* (Amherst, N.Y.: Prometheus Books, 1989), p. 201.

10. The same word which the King James version has translated as "flying, creeping things," the word *oph,* is used at least eighteen times in the book of Genesis to refer to birds. But in Leviticus 11:22 locusts, beetles, and grasshoppers are given as examples of creatures in this class. There are no four-legged flying creatures.

11. In 1983 the Vatican admitted its mistreatment of Galileo; it admitted that his view is correct in 1992.

12. Thomas Paine, *The Age of Reason* (Amherst, N.Y.: Prometheus Books, 1984), pp. 114 and 115, respectively.

Question #5

Don't Reports of Miracles Prove That God Exists?

A miracle is a violation of the laws of nature because of supernatural influence. Although miracles are often cited as evidence of a god, there are major obstacles to the successful use of this approach. Some of the many possible objections are the following: (A) testimony about a miracle is never sufficient justification for belief that such an event really occurred; (B) even if it were granted that a seemingly miraculous event has occurred in a given circumstance, this would not be evidence for god's existence; and (C) there is no evidence that miracles have occurred.

A. Testimony of a miracle does not establish that such an event occurred.

Christians often cite reports of miracles as evidence that god exists. In such cases, section X of David Hume's *An Enquiry Con-*

125

cerning Human Understanding should be required reading. Hume makes a strong case that testimony of a miracle is never enough to justify belief that a miracle actually occurred. As Hume noted, the testimony of another person cannot be considered extraordinary evidence, which is what would be needed to show that a miracle had indeed occurred.

The laws of nature are generalizations of observed events which describe the forces of the universe. As scientists have encountered events that could not be explained by natural law, the laws have been amended. The history of science is the history of scientific revolution after revolution as the old ideas are shown to be inadequate and new theories come along to replace those that are obsolete. As Hume explains, human experience and observation establish the laws of nature. Those held to be most basic, such as the law of gravity, are established by our consistent life experience. For example, it is our experience that unsupported objects that are heavier than air, near the surface of the earth, and not subject to the influence of magnets, will fall. The law, the generalization, is created to describe a consistent class of events. When we are faced with a choice between believing two conflicting things, we ought to choose what most conforms to our experience. Preference should be given to believing that the law of nature holds simply because, by definition, it is the description of a consistent class of events.

For example, suppose that someone claims that a holy man floated in midair because he was in a trance. Confronted with the choice between believing that everyone has been incorrect about gravity or that the person reporting the event is either mistaken or lying, the choice is clear. There are no known instances of the law of gravity being violated in this way, but there are many instances in human history where people have lied or been mistaken about certain facts. Thus, it is most consistent with what is known about the world to believe that the person reporting the supposed miracle

126

is either mistaken or lying. Without further evidence, the mere account of the incident is not enough to overturn the well-established law of nature.

Most religious believers agree, in fact, that testimony alone is *not* sufficient to show that a miracle has occurred. Other religions besides Christianity also claim miracles, but Christians don't consider reports of Hindu miracles as proof that the Hindu gods exist. In most cases Christians would not even believe that the miracle occurred. Reports of miracles in the Christian tradition should be treated in the same way. They are insufficient evidence.

Testimony alone does not establish that a miracle has occurred.

B. A seemingly miraculous event would not be evidence for the existence of gods.

Even if a supposed miracle is witnessed, this would not show that gods exist.

1. It cannot be shown that an event is a violation of the laws of nature.

There are two good reasons to believe that it could never be shown that any given event is a violation of the laws of nature.

a. *The laws of nature are not known completely.*

In order to show that the laws of nature have been violated, all the laws of nature would have to be known. However, it is recognized by even the best scientists that much remains to be found out about the workings of nature. To say that the laws of nature have been violated is to say that human beings will never discover a law of nature which would explain the observed event. Given how rapidly science has advanced just in the last one hundred years, it is surely foolhardy to make such blanket statements about what science will or will not discover. There may be an unknown force of nature at work; there may be a regular, predictable phenomenon which resulted in the supposed miracle, a regularity of nature which has just not been observed often enough to be formulated into a law.

Furthermore, it could be the case that the laws of nature are simply not uniform. Perhaps it is the natural course of things that certain laws of nature are in effect most of the time, but at certain times they are not. If this were the case, then such laws could be "violated" because, as quantum physics suggests, they are causally operative statistically, such as 80 percent of the time, but not continuously. It is known that some laws operate in this way on the subatomic level.

Because we do not know all about how natural forces work, one cannot show that a given event was not due to natural forces.

b. *There are always alternative explanations for a supposed miracle.*

When faced with the observation of a supposed miracle, there are always alternative explanations besides the conclusion that the laws of nature have been violated. Not only could there be unknown forces at work, as explained above, but there could be

128

unusual circumstances present which allow *known* laws to produce unusual results. Some readers may recall the television series *The Flying Nun* in which actress Sally Field could become airborne when wearing her unusual nun's habit because of the laws of aerodynamics. The premise for this show was that, although the natural laws in question were not violated, this nun's particular costume, body weight, and shape, combined with the windspeed, allowed unusual results from well-known laws. Could someone ever completely rule out in the case of a supposed miracle that there may have been an unusual combination of circumstances which resulted in a unique but natural occurrence?

In addition, rather than conclude that a god exists because of the report or observation of a supposed miracle, one could conclude that there could be *other* forces at work besides gods. There could be a group of technologically advanced beings playing a trick on humans to see how they would react. Anyone who has seen a few episodes of *Star Trek* can see how this objection could be explained in detail.

If the theist cannot rule out the clever alien scenario, as we saw with the issue of biblical prophecy, then from the claim that a miracle has seemingly occurred the conclusion that a god is responsible does not follow. Suppose that a believer in clever space aliens witnessed a supposed miracle and asserted that this is evidence that such beings exist. Would the theist allow that the conclusion follows? Of course not. Then neither can anyone allow that the conclusion that a god exists follows from a supposed miracle. Each must eliminate rival theories as impossible or unlikely before establishing their preferred conclusion. Almost any other proposed explanation for a seeming miracle would be more likely to be true than theism because the other claims would not assert the existence of a supreme being, a situation which would place the theistic proposal at a great disadvantage.

Unless alternative explanations can be eliminated as possibilities, the theist cannot legitimately claim, *even if a miracle did seem to occur,* that gods exist. The conclusion does not follow. It is unlikely that a theist, who makes the exceedingly strong claim that a god exists, could ever show that other possible explanations for a supposed miracle are impossible or less likely than the theistic hypothesis.

2. It cannot be shown that an event is due to supernatural influence.

Even if it somehow could be determined that an event violated the laws of nature, this would not prove that there are gods. Gods are usually thought to bring about events by magic powers, by uttering certain words, and it could never be established that these events, the uttering of certain words or the willing of an event to happen, preceded the supposed miracle. Of course, it is even less likely that anyone could show that any particular god is responsible for a given miraculous event. Some religions have gods who enjoy playing tricks. Could a Christian ever show that a miracle was *not* due to the mischief of some other religion's god?

In order to show that a miracle has occurred, the theist must show that the relevant law of nature is in effect continuously, that no alternative explanation is possible, and that the given law of nature has been violated due to supernatural influence. It is unlikely that this could ever be shown.

C. There is no evidence that miracles have occurred.

With regard to both reports of miracles in the bible and those of extrabiblical miracles, no report of a supposed miracle has established that such an event actually occurred.

1. Biblical claims about miracles may be dismissed.

Previous remarks about the reliability of the bible should suffice to show that the bible cannot be considered a reliable document, so it certainly cannot be considered strong evidence that a miracle has occurred.

2. No claim about extrabiblical miracles has been shown to hold up under careful examination.

An organization called the Committee for the Scientific Investigation of Claims of the Paranormal (CSICOP) investigates claims about paranormal activity. They investigate reports of statues that are said to cry and of people who are reported to float in the air, those who claim to be able to dowse for water, have out-of-body experiences, obtain knowledge by extrasensory perception, and perform other such feats. Some of the best minds in the various fields of science belong to this organization. This organization and others, as well as a number of individuals (such as the magicians Harry Houdini and James "The Amazing" Randi) have investigated claims of miracles and paranormal events for decades. *No such claim has ever held up under scrutiny.* Investigators have found either that the reports of such claims were unreliable, the person making the claim was caught engaging in deception, the report was mistaken, or a naturalistic explanation for the phenomenon was found. For example, statues in India recently reported to be miraculously drinking milk were found to be quite ordinary statues which allowed the milk to flow from the "mouth" of the statue by capillary action due to the material used in their construction. A purely natural explanation was found.

Many widely reported "miraculous" occurrences such as the Shroud of Turin and Mexico's Image of Guadalupe painting have been *proven* to be frauds. In the case of the shroud, for example, the Catholic Church not only denounced the shroud as a fraud when it first appeared, a Bishop Pierre d'Arcis reported to the pope in 1389 that he had even found the artist who had created it! Weeping icons, the blood of St. Januaris, stigmata, faith healing, and similar supposed miracles have been investigated in detail and shown to be *completely worthless* as evidence for the occurrence of a miracle.

Reports of children seeing the Virgin Mary and other such visions are also worthless as evidence. At best, in these cases the so-called miracle is actually the report of a miracle, not a miracle itself. What can be observed is merely someone's testimony. The person is claiming to be seeing or hearing something, but it cannot be determined whether this report is accurate. There may be causes which could explain the report, causes of which others are unaware. The person reporting the vision may be subject to physical or chemical changes due to some as yet undiscovered subjective state. For example, the ergot fungus *Claviceps purpurea*, which often infects rye and other grains, can cause hallucinations and other psychedelic

132

effects. It is thought that eating bread contaminated with this or some similar fungus may have been responsible for some of the claims about witches and other odd behavior in Salem, Massachusetts, in 1692. Can hallucinations, mental illness, or lying ever be ruled out as an explanation where the *only* "evidence" is someone's testimony?

Many mystics who report visions first starve or abuse themselves to such an extent that they are no longer reliable witnesses because their faculties are impaired. As Bertrand Russell noted:

> From a scientific point of view, we can make no distinction between the man who eats little and sees heaven and the man who drinks much and sees snakes. Each is in an abnormal physical condition and therefore has abnormal perceptions.[1]

At worst, the report of a vision is merely a lie. Because there is *no way* to distinguish between an accurate report (if such were possible), one that is an honest mistake, or one that is an outright lie, the report is worthless as evidence.

Conclusion

A. Testimony of a miracle does not establish that such an event occurred.
B. A seemingly miraculous event would not be evidence for the existence of gods.
   1. It cannot be shown that an event is a violation of the laws of nature.
   2. It cannot be shown that an event is due to supernatural influence.

C. There is no evidence that miracles have occurred.
  1. Biblical claims about miracles may be dismissed.
  2. No claim about extrabiblical miracles has been shown to hold up under careful examination.

Therefore, reports of miracles do not prove that gods exist.

It should be of concern to believers that no claim about a miracle has ever been able to pass careful examination, but it should be equally troubling that widespread fraud and deception on the part of faith healers, the clergy, and others who have an interest in the promotion of religious ideas, has been proven from time to time throughout the history of Christianity. The Church father Eusebius actively promoted fraud and deception in order to further Church interests. Even today faith healers have been shown to be charlatans. Perhaps believers should ask themselves why truth needs to be promoted by falsehood. Is their god so unable to reveal himself to human beings that his followers must resort to lies?

Before acknowledging that a miracle has occurred, perhaps believers should reserve judgment about the event until unbiased, expert witnesses can investigate and publish their findings. The general public is too quick to label anything from a burnt tortilla to an oil stain an example of a miracle.

Note

1. Bertrand Russell, *Religion and Science* (Oxford: Oxford University Press, 1935), p. 188.

Question #6

Aren't There Philosophical Proofs Which Demonstrate That God Exists?

There are many so-called proofs of god's existence, none of which survives review by one with some skill in critical thinking. The two most popular arguments are the argument from design and the cosmological argument. Each of these arguments attempts to use some observation or conclusion about the world as a foundation for its conclusion that god must exist. I will explain the content of the most common forms of these arguments, and then I will mention some of the reasons that they fail.

A. The argument from design fails.

The argument from design, also called the *teleological argument,* is a popular avenue of argument for those who attempt to prove that god exists.

Implicit in the argument from design is the following principle:

The "Order Implies a Designer" Principle (OID)—
Any object or system which shows evidence of order must
be the result of intelligent design.

The argument from design not only requires this principle, it requires that the principle be true without exception. If there could be an exception to the principle, that is, order which is not the result of intelligent design, then the order of the universe could be an exception and the argument would fail.

1. The argument from design compares the universe to an artifact.

The argument from design usually begins with the statement that the workings of the universe, the interaction of natural laws, the movement of heavenly bodies, the accurate function of human organs, and other systems that seem to function in an orderly way resemble the mechanism of artifacts. Theist William Paley devised the following example. If you were walking along and found a watch on the ground, you would know, by examining it, that it must have had a designer. It is too intricate, its parts work together too well, for it to be the case that such a thing occurred by chance. Similarly, the example suggests, when we look around at the universe, which is so much grander than the watch, how much more certain we can be that this marvelous mechanism, the universe, must have a designer! The universe could not have come about by chance, concludes the theist. Further, its designer must be extremely intelligent, perhaps omniscient, and incredibly powerful. Surely this is the only explanation for the existence of the universe. There must be a designer, and this designer is god.

2. There are decisive objections to the argument from design.

Unfortunately, an examination of this line of reasoning shows that the argument does not even come close to establishing its conclusion. There are many objections to the argument. Below is a small sampling of some of these.

a. Order does, in fact, come from disorder.

A book by physicist Victor Stenger, *Not By Design*, should be carefully studied by anyone interested in using the argument from design.[1] Stenger shows how it is quite common for order to be generated out of chaos, and that this is a corollary of contemporary physical theories. Order can be generated by chance even on a computer programmed to generate random dots on a screen. Designs form, patterns are recognized. In addition, complex structures can, by computer models, be shown to result from even the simplest rules. The notion that order cannot come into existence without an intelligent designer, a principle crucial to the argument from design, can thus be shown to be false, and the design argument fails.

b. The theist is forced to deny that order must be the result of intelligent design.

Order can only come from intelligent design, holds the theist; it cannot be the product of chaos or chance. Moreover, god must have been well-ordered and intelligent to have been able to create the ordered universe. But then, if order can only come from design, on the OID principle, god, who is also ordered, must have been the result of yet *another* designer who is even more intelligent, and

137

that designer must have been the product of design, too, and so on *ad infinitum*. Yet the theist denies this. The theist asserts that god, who is not chaotic, and who is well-ordered, was *not* the result of intelligent design. Thus, the theist denies the OID principle which is at the core of the argument from design. Once the theist admits that it is false that order is always the result of intelligent design, the whole argument from design collapses.

c. The argument from design is based on an extremely weak analogy.

The argument from design is an argument by analogy. The more similarities between the analogates (the things compared), the stronger the analogy, and, consequently, the stronger the argument. The fewer similarities, the weaker the argument. Important to the argument from design, then, is the number of similarities between the analogates. In this case, the analogates are human artifacts and the universe. How much do they have in common?

All the artifacts in our experience have been made of preexisting material. If the universe is like an artifact, then, it must have been made of preexisting material. But the theist denies this and claims that god created the universe *ex nihilo*, out of nothing.

All the artifacts we have seen have been built by beings with physical bodies. Thus we may conclude that the universe was built by a being with a physical body. But the theist denies that god has a physical body.

Our experience with artifacts shows that they are built by labor, by physically moving material together or apart. Thus, we should conclude, if the universe is like an artifact, that it was built by labor. However, the theist, especially the Christian, denies this and says that the entire universe was created by god uttering magic words (see Genesis, chapter 1).

Large and complex ships, houses, buildings, and other constructions are built by groups of people working together. Thus, the universe, if it is like a large and complex artifact, must have been built by many gods working together. But the theist denies this. Polytheists, perhaps, would not deny this.

If an artifact has flaws, one can conclude either that the designer or builder was ignorant, sloppy, or just did not care about the outcome enough to put more work into it. The universe has stars explode and collide; there are earthquakes, floods, volcanic eruptions, hurricanes, and other natural disasters which cause huge loss of life, and which are not in any way caused by human action; there are genetic disorders such as spina bifida which kill humans and cause intense agony; there have been several worldwide extinctions in the past which resulted in the deaths of 90 percent or more of the species existing in the world at that time, and so on. Thus, we may conclude that god was either ignorant, sloppy, or just did not care enough about the outcome to make the universe any better than it is. But the theist denies this.

There are many other disanalogies between the universe and an artifact, but it should now be clear that the theist denies that the universe is like an artifact in many important ways. Thus, the analogy between the universe and an artifact seems to be simply the result of the theist's selection of one aspect of what we know of artifacts—that they are often orderly—and the denial of many other characteristics about artifacts. The theist must admit that the universe and artifacts are more dissimilar than similar. Since the theist makes the analogy only with regard to a *single* trait, the analogy between an artifact and the universe is *incredibly weak*, and, as a result, so is the argument as a whole.

d. The conclusion of the argument does not follow from the analogy.

Even if it were granted, for the sake of argument, that the universe was created as the result of design, it still could not be concluded from this alone that the traditional god is the creator of the universe. The argument is thus logically invalid, and for this reason alone it may be safely rejected. The argument is invalid because the conclusion does not follow from the premises. The Christian wishes to conclude that there was a single creator of the universe and that this is the Christian god, a creator who is, among other things, omnipotent (all-powerful), omniscient (all-knowing), omnibenevolent (all-good), and transcendent (outside of space and time), but it cannot be shown that those other characteristics are required for creating the universe. The argument falls far short of its goal.

(i) The argument does not show that there was a single creator.

One could not conclude, for example, that the creator had to be a single being as opposed to billions of beings. The *most* that the design argument can show is that there was *at least one* creator of the universe. This does not say who or how many creators there were. Of course, the argument cannot even conclude this much, in light of other objections.

(ii) The argument does not show that the creator still exists.

The design argument does not show, in any way, that, if there were a creator or creators of the universe, the creator(s) still exist(s). There is no reason to reject the idea that even *if* the universe was created, the creator died in the process. There are many examples in our experience of creations outlasting their creators. The pyramids in Egypt have outlasted their builders. There is no reason to suppose that the builder of the universe, even if it were granted that there was one, must still exist. *At best*, the design argument would show that at one time there was at least one creator of the universe.

(iii) The argument does not show that the creator was omnipotent.

It does not follow that, if there were a creator of the universe, the creator had to be omnipotent (all-powerful), since it is not known how much power is needed to create the universe. We don't know how universes are made, so it would be irrational to assume that only an omnipotent being could create a universe. In fact, some current theories in physics suggest that if the positive energy of the universe, the matter, is exactly equal to the negative energy, the expansion of the matter of the universe, then the positive and negative energy would cancel each other, and the sum of the energy of the universe would be equal to zero. This means that it would have taken *no energy* whatsoever to create the universe. Since this is a possible explanation, it shows that one does *not* have to conclude that only an omnipotent being could create the universe. As long as there is at least one alternative to the theistic explanation of the origin of the universe, the design argument is unsuccessful.

(iv) The argument does not show that the creator was omnibenevolent.

The design argument does not show that the creator of the universe, if any, must be omnibenevolent (all-good). Being able to create a universe has nothing to do with being moral. The design argument cannot even show that the creator cannot be omnimalevolent (all-evil).

(v) The argument does not show that the creator was omniscient.

How intelligent does one need to be to make a universe? What is required? Since no one knows, one cannot conclude that the creator, if any, was omniscient. Omniscience is another attribute which cannot be derived from the argument from design.

Since the conclusion does not follow from the supposed evidence, the argument clearly rests on a faulty line of reasoning. Those with even a little familiarity with the basic principles of logic will recognize that the discovery of invalidity spells death to any argument.

Summary of section A

There are other objections to the design argument, but the considerations mentioned here should be enough to show that the argument does not establish its conclusion. The argument is based on the principle that order is always the product of intelligent design, a principle which can be shown to be false, and which even the theist denies. The argument is also based on a weak analogy. Finally, the argument is logically invalid; and the conclusion that the thing which created the universe, if there were such a thing, had attributes such as omniscience, omnipotence, omnibenevolence, and related characteristics does not follow from the premises. These considerations show that the argument from design does not

142

work, and the argument may be dismissed as a failure. In fact, the argument from design is so riddled with flaws that it may be used as an effective argument *against* theism! The analogy between artifacts and the universe makes the theistic explanation implausible.[2]

B. The cosmological argument fails.

There are different versions of the cosmological argument. All involve stating some fact about the world which is causally related to some other fact, which is also, in turn, causally related to some other fact, and so on. It is then suggested that this chain of facts could only be explained or started by something other than the individual members of the chain, and this explanation is god.

Implicit in any cosmological argument is the Principle of Sufficient Reason. This principle may be stated in different ways, one of which is the following:

> **The Principle of Sufficient Reason (PSR)**—Anything that happens or which is always caused to happen or to exist.

In other words, you can't get something from nothing, and things don't happen without a cause or reason. This principle is a general version of principles used in each of the three arguments below.

1. Aquinas uses the facts of motion and causation in his arguments.

St. Thomas Aquinas (1225–1274) used a number of approaches to try to prove the existence of god. His five methods of attempting to prove that god exists, the foundations of which he owes to Aristotle, are generally known as his Five Ways. Two of Aquinas' strongest arguments, from his *Summa Theologica*, will be examined.[3] Aquinas uses observations about motion and causation as an important part of two of his cosmological arguments. These versions can be summarized as follows:

a. Aquinas' First Way involves a chain of motion.

1) Some things move.
2) For anything that moves, its movement must be caused by something other than itself. In other words, if a given thing, call it "A," moves, its motion must be caused by something else in motion, call it "B." The motion of the thing "B" must also be moved by some other moving thing "C," and so on.
3) It is impossible for this chain of movers to be an infinite regress.
4) Therefore, there was a first mover which does not itself move, but which moved at least one other thing. This first mover is god.

b. Aquinas' Second Way involves a chain of causes.

1) Some things are caused.
2) For anything which is caused, its cause must be something other than itself. In other words, if a given thing, call it "A,"

is caused, its existence must be caused by something else which exists, call it "B." The existence of the thing "B" must also be caused by some other thing "C," and so on.

3) It is impossible for this chain of causes to be an infinite regress.

4) Therefore, there was a first cause which was not itself caused, but which caused something else. This first cause is god.

Aquinas believed that reflection upon the origin of motion and causation was enough to prove that god must exist.

2. Another popular version of the cosmological argument involves the concept of a necessary being.

Another version of the cosmological argument, called the *Kalam cosmological argument,* enjoys much popularity among Christian apologists (defenders). The name derives from the Kalam school of Islamic thought which developed this version of the argument. They got the argument from sixth-century Christians. This version uses a distinction between contingent beings and necessary beings.

Contingent beings are those which are caused to exist by something other than themselves. People, for example, are caused to exist by their parents, so they are contingent beings. Tables, chairs, and houses are contingent beings. A necessary being, however, is not caused to exist by another being. A necessary being is caused to exist by its own nature. It is the sort of being who *must* exist; a necessary being cannot fail to exist. The nonexistence of a necessary being, on this view, is a logical contradiction. If one accepts the Principle of Sufficient Reason (PSR) and the concept of necessary beings, then one can formulate this version of the argument.

The Kalam cosmological argument:

1) There now exist contingent beings.
2) Either there has always been a continuous chain of contingent beings infinitely into the past, *or* the chain of contingent beings began at some point.
3) It is impossible that there has always been a continuous chain of contingent beings infinitely into the past.
4) Therefore, the chain of contingent beings began at some point.
5) Anything that begins to exist has a cause of its existence.
6) The only possible cause of the chain of contingent beings is a necessary being.
7) Therefore, a necessary being exists. This necessary being is god.

3. There are decisive objections to the cosmological argument.

Although the arguments summarized above have been historically influential, there have been equally influential, and philosophically powerful, objections to them. In fact, these objections have never been successfully rebutted. In the discussion below, for brevity, let "First Thing" represent the first mover, first cause, and the necessary being from each of the arguments above. "The chain" will refer to the relevant set of causally dependent movers, causes, and contingent beings.

a. The arguments are invalid.

What one should note first about these arguments is that they are invalid. This means that even if the supporting premises were true, the conclusion would not follow from them.

(i) Even if it were the case that the chain could not go back infinitely far, it would not follow that there had to be only one First Thing. At best, the argument would show that there must have been *at least one* First Thing. There is no way to reduce the number of First Things from one million, or even a billion or more. That there was *only* one First Thing does not follow.

(ii) The cosmological argument may conclude, at best, that at least one thing has had an effect on some other thing. However, it does not follow from Aquinas' arguments that the first cause or mover must still exist. Aquinas' arguments show, at best, that at some time in the past at least one thing existed. There is no reason to think that something which was the agent of causation or motion in the distant past would have to exist at the present time. Many things that caused other things to happen in the past do not exist now, at least not in the same form. The food that sustained Abraham Lincoln when he was ten years old had causal powers then, but we don't conclude from that fact that an apple he ate then must exist at the present time. Something which acted on something else in the past need not exist now, so Aquinas' arguments do not show anything about the present.

(iii) It does not follow from the cosmological argument that the First Thing must be omnipotent. The cosmological arguments show, at best, that something in the past was moved or caused to exist. Nothing is shown about what it was that was moved or caused. The arguments cannot show that the effect of motion or causation was anything more than a subatomic particle. In fact, current theories in physics suggest that many particles are so small

147

and have so little mass that they may be acted upon by exceedingly minute fluctuations of energy. There is no reason to believe that something must be omnipotent in order to have an effect on a sub-atomic particle, and such a minute effect is the most that the cosmological argument can show.

(iv) It does not follow from the premises that the First Thing had to be conscious, or even alive. There are many instances in nature of causation due to substances or objects which are inanimate. Chemicals, for example, may react strongly when mixed even though they are not alive. A tornado can level a building without being alive. There is no reason to think that the First Cause, if any, was a living or conscious being. Causation does not require consciousness.

(v) It does not follow from this argument that the First Thing must be omnibenevolent. There is no reason to believe that something must be all-good in order to have causal powers. Since it cannot even be shown that the First Thing had to have been alive or conscious, there is even less reason to suppose that the First Thing was omnibenevolent.

(vi) It does not follow from the cosmological argument that the First Thing must be omniscient. It is well-known in physics that agents of causation and motion need not even be alive, so the conclusion that the First Thing must have been all-knowing is absurd. There is no reason to conclude that an unknown something which acted upon another unknown something at some unknown point in the past must have been all-knowing or even aware of what was happening. The conclusion is not warranted.

Similarly, with regard to the other characteristics that the theist usually wishes to ascribe to god, it does not follow from the cosmological argument that the First Thing has such properties. Clearly, this line of reasoning does not result in the conclusion which the Christian desires, so the cosmological argument does not work. Even if the argument could show that there was a First Thing, it does not show that this thing had any of the attributes ascribed to the theistic god.

b. *It cannot be shown that an infinite regress is impossible.*

In order to establish the conclusion of the argument (if the argument were valid), the theist would have to support the premise which asserts that the chain cannot go back infinitely far. Philosophers such as Aquinas have simply assumed that everyone would agree that such a regress is impossible, but for the argument to be a proof we must know that its premises are true. If we do not know that this third premise of each of these arguments is true, then the argument does not establish its conclusion.

(i) Some apologists have suggested that an infinite regress is impossible because an infinite amount of time would need to have passed in order to get to the present, and, they add, an infinite series cannot be traversed. To traverse means to begin at some point and travel point by point to another point, and these theists hold that this could never be done with an infinite regress.

(A) One response to this is simply that there is no given moment of time which is infinitely distant from the present. For any given moment in the past, call it "T," that moment is a finite number of moments from the present. Since there is no infinitely distant point at which to begin, any given point in the past *could* be traversed to the present. Often theists respond, however, by suggesting that there are moments in time more distant than T and that what they meant was that these more distant moments are infinitely distant. But, again, there is no such moment T-prime which is infinitely distant from the present—or from T, at whatever moment in time T is.

(B) But, protests the theist, what is meant are those moments in time further back, at the beginning of your proposed time line. The obvious response here is that, by hypothesis, the time line *has no beginning*, since the objection is the possibility of an infinite regress, so the theist has no case. One who objects to the cosmological argument by suggesting that an infinite regress is possible is not asserting that any infinite series was started and traversed. There is no beginning in an infinite regress; one does not begin to traverse it. By hypothesis, one has *always been* "traversing" it— the trip has always been in progress. It was never begun—this is implicit in the suggestion of an infinite regress. Given this hypothesis, it is merely question-begging to state that the regress had to begin at some point in order for it to be traversed. The theist simply misunderstands what is being suggested.

If it is possible that there have always been moments in time, then there is no problem in concluding that there may have been an infinite regress of events which has led to the present.

(ii) Attempts by some theologians to show that the concept of an infinite regress leads to logical contradictions are a waste of time. Most of these attempts are painfully transparent demonstrations of logical fallacies. In any event, mathematicians have been working with both positive and negative integers (an infinite regress) for centuries without encountering contradictions, so there is no conceptual absurdity in supposing that an infinite regress is possible.

The *possibility* of such a regress is all that is needed to derail this crucial premise of the cosmological argument, since the impossibility of such a regress is required for this argument for theism to be successful. If the theist cannot prove that an infinite regress is impossible, then the cosmological argument fails as a proof. No theist has ever been able to show that an infinite regress is impossible.

c. The concept of a necessary being is incoherent.

It is not clear what is meant by a being whose nature guarantees that it will always exist. Hume asserted: "Whatever we conceive as existent, we can also conceive as nonexistent. There is no being, therefore, whose nonexistence implies a contradiction."[4]

Hume concluded, correctly, that the words "necessary existence" have no meaning. No theist has ever been able to explain how such a thing as a necessary being could exist or what about such a being makes its existence necessary. Human beings have neither the experience of such beings nor the explanation of such beings. The more one demands an explanation for such beings, and the more one hears the evasive answer from the theist, the more one is inclined to think that the theist holds that necessary beings exist by some sort of magic power. Until a clear concept of what such beings are or an explanation of how they could exist is presented, the concept is rightly considered incoherent and explanatorily impotent. Versions of the cosmological argument and other theistic arguments which use the concept of a necessary being may be considered unsuccessful.

d. The First Thing could be the universe itself.

Even if the cosmological argument did show, in one of its versions, that a necessary being had to exist, or that there had to be a first causer or mover, that first thing or necessary being could have simply been the universe itself. This explanation is simpler than the explanation that god *and* the universe exist. The simpler view is more likely to be true than its rival, since the "universe only" model assumes less than the other model. For any two rival theories, all other things being equal, the theory with fewer assumptions has the greater probability of being true. This is a principle accepted in science and philosophy, and with good reason.

Consider the following example. Suppose that two people—call them A and B—enter the lobby of a building. A says, "There is an elephant in the basement of this building," and B says, "There is an elephant *and a spotted llama* in the basement of this building." Because A and B each claim that there is an elephant, but B claims more than that, the probability that A is correct is higher than the probability that B is correct. Why? B can't be right without A also being correct, since, if there is a llama and an elephant in the basement, B would be correct, and the presence of the elephant would make A correct, too. But A *can* be correct *without* B being correct. If there is only an elephant, or if there is an elephant and a pig, or an elephant and a goat, then A is correct but B is incorrect. It is easy to see, then, that more possible circumstances would make A's assertion correct than would make B's correct, so the simpler assertion has a greater probability of being correct.

The assertion that only the universe exists is simpler than the assertion that the universe *and god* exist, so the former claim has a greater chance of being true. Thus, if one must claim that there was a first cause, a first mover, or a necessary being, one would be more likely to be correct if one said that the First Thing was the universe itself than if one said that both god *and* the universe exist.

e. The Principle of Sufficient Reason cannot be shown to be true.

The Principle of Sufficient Reason (PSR) is used in some form or another in all versions of the cosmological argument. Aquinas' versions used modified forms of this principle. He states that things which are caused must be caused by something else, that things which move must be moved by something else. There must be a reason that these things happen. They cannot happen for no reason, he assumes. The PSR is explicit in the Kalam version of the argument explained above.

Note that for the cosmological argument to work, the principle must not only be true, it must be true without exception. If an exception is allowed, if it is granted that things can sometimes happen or exist for no reason, then the argument fails because there need not be a being at the origin of these chains which purports to serve as the explanation for the chain. The whole point of a cosmological argument is to show that there is some chain of causes or movers which cannot be explained by any member of the chain itself, and there must be an explanation, a cause, of some sort. The explanation proposed is god. If the PSR cannot be defended, then the argument cannot work. Can this principle be defended?

It cannot.

(i) We cannot know that the PSR is true.

We cannot know that the PSR is true *a priori*, by reason alone. There is no contradiction in supposing that something can occur for no reason, so we cannot find out the truth of the PSR by simply examining the concepts involved.

Further, we cannot show that the PSR is true by observation or experience. We cannot watch a bunch of nothings to see if something ever comes out of them. We cannot appeal to our everyday experience for confirmation that things occur for a reason because this would not show that the principle is true without exception.

Since we cannot know that the PSR is true by observation or by reason alone, then it would seem that we cannot know that it is true, and the cosmological argument fails.

(ii) There are good reasons to believe that the PSR is false.

In addition to being unable to show that the PSR is true, the theist must admit that there is solid scientific evidence that the PSR is false. The prevailing model in physics is that of quantum theory. This is the field of physics devoted to exploring the subatomic realm. Because of its unprecedented precision and its unexpected discoveries, the principles formulated in this branch of science have led to major revisions formulated in this branch of science have led to major revisions of theories of matter, time, causality, and the limits of human knowledge. Quantum physics is the most successful theory of physics ever conceived, and there is a wealth of evidence, both observational and theoretical, in its favor. In *Quantum Reality*, Nick Herbert writes:

> Quantum theory continued . . . to prosper beyond its inventors' wildest dreams, resolving subtle problems of atomic structure, tackling the nucleus some ten thousand times smaller than the atom itself, and then extending its reach to the realm of elementary particles (quarks, gluons, leptons) which many believe to be the world's ultimate constituents. With each success quantum theory became more audacious. . . . Heaping success upon success, quantum theory boldly exposes itself to potential falsification on a thousand different fronts. Its record is impressive: quantum theory passes every test we can devise. After sixty years of play, this theory is still batting a thousand.[5]

The success of this theory of physics cannot be disputed.

The proof of quantum physics is proof that some facts have no explanation. Quantum physics implies that there is *no* reason for the decay of a given atomic nucleus at a particular time. This is solid evidence against the PSR. In *The Cosmic Code: Quantum*

Physics As the Language of Nature, physicist Heinz R. Pagels, using the term "God" figuratively, explains the depth of quantum indeterminacy:

> Not only must human experimenters give up ever knowing when a particular atom is going to radiate or a particular nucleus undergo radioactive decay, but these events are even unknown in the perfect mind of God. . . . Even God can give you only the odds for some events to occur, not certainty.[6]

> But is there a possibility that beyond quantum theory there exists a new, deterministic physics, described by some kind of subquantum theory. . . ? According to quantum theory this is not possible. . . . The very act of attempting to establish determinism produces indeterminism. There is no randomness like quantum randomness. Like us, God plays dice—He, too, knows only the odds.[7]

The evidence for the indeterminacy of some events is evidence that the PSR is false.

Since we cannot know that the PSR is true, and we have good reason to believe that the PSR is false, and the cosmological argument depends on the PSR, the cosmological argument is in serious trouble to say the least.

Summary of section B

It has been shown that there are major difficulties with the cosmological argument. The arguments are invalid, and this alone should cause them to be dismissed. The assertion that there cannot be an infinite regress of causes or movers is unsupported. Versions of the argument which use the concept of a necessary being cannot explain the nature of this concept. The supposition that the universe itself was the First Thing is more likely to be true than the assertion that god and the universe exist. Finally, the argument depends on the Principle of Sufficient Reason, and this principle cannot be defended. Clearly, the cosmological argument fails.

While there are other versions of the cosmological argument, none has been successful. All of them use the PSR or some version of it, and all are invalid insofar as they do not show that god exists. They show, *at best*, that at least one thing with very limited attributes exists or once existed, and all are subject to objections similar to those given against the three versions of the argument we have seen.

Conclusion

Decisive objections to the argument from design and the cosmological argument suggest that neither accomplishes its objective. Throughout human history, theologians have advanced other arguments which attempt to prove the existence of god, and others calculated simply to show that the existence of god is rational or probable. Without exception, all have failed. Michael Martin's *Atheism: A Philosophical Justification* is, perhaps, the best scholarly survey of the most popular of these arguments which shows how and why they do not succeed.

Notes

1. Victor J. Stenger, *Not by Design* (Amherst, N.Y.: Prometheus Books, 1988).

2. See Michael Martin, *Atheism: A Philosophical Justification* (Philadelphia: Temple University Press, 1990), chapter 13.

3. St. Thomas Aquinas, *Introduction to St. Thomas Aquinas,* Anton C. Pegis, ed. (New York: The Modern Library, 1948), pp. 25–26.

4. David Hume, *Dialogues Concerning Natural Religion and the Posthumous Essays,* Richard H. Popkin, ed. (Indianapolis, Ind.: Hackett Publishing Co., 1985), p. 55.

5. Nick Herbert, *Quantum Reality: Beyond the New Physics* (Garden City, N.Y.: Doubleday, 1985), p. 94.

6. Heinz R. Pagels, *The Cosmic Code: Quantum Physics As the Language of Nature* (New York: Simon and Schuster, 1982), p. 83.

7. Ibid., p. 86.

Question #7

Wouldn't Someone Have to Know Everything in Order to Say That There Is No God?

Theists often state that someone would have to know everything in order to say that there is no god. This approach is sometimes used in an attempt to persuade the atheist to "give" a little on his or her position. The intent here seems to be the vain hope of narrowing the gap between atheism and theism by trying to show that it is irrational to be an atheist (one who denies that god exists), and that, at best, one can be an agnostic (one who suspends judgment about whether or not there is a god). The theist will insist that one may, perhaps, be able to declare that one does not know that god exists, but one cannot deny the existence of god because, unless one knows *all* the things in the universe, there may be some unknown thing that could turn out to be god.

Unfortunately, this approach will not work. There are many ways to respond to this charge. Some of them are: (A) atheism in the absence of evidence is an accepted principle; (B) the concept of god is incoherent, so god *cannot* exist; (C) the existence of evil is strong evidence against the existence of the traditional god; and

(D) the existence of nonbelievers is evidence against the existence of the traditional god. Each of these four responses shows how one can legitimately conclude that god does not exist without requiring one first to be omniscient.

A. Atheism in the absence of evidence is an accepted principle.

Most people believe that it is a good principle of common sense to refrain from believing something extraordinary until evidence is presented in favor of that claim. In the case of supernatural claims, we can call this the presumption of atheism—the principle of disbelief in the absence of evidence. If this principle is correct, then a good case can be made that one can say that god does not exist.

1. There is a presumption of atheism.

Most people believe that it is common sense that one should believe that an extraordinary claim is false until strong evidence is produced in its favor. Most people believe that one should believe that a god does *not* exist until there is evidence that the god does exist.

a. Extraordinary claims require evidence in order to be believed.

Let us define "extraordinary claim" as one requiring you to give up some of your present commonsense beliefs in order to believe the claim. By "evidence" I mean some positive grounds for belief in a conclusion, and the grounds may be either conceptual (in the form of arguments) or physical (in cases of claims about historical events, for example). Credible evidence is grounds for belief which is obtained through a reliable method and which confers likelihood of truth upon a conclusion. By "evidence" in the following discussion it will be understood that what is meant is credible evidence.

What is an example of an extraordinary claim? If I were to tell you that I had eaten a peanut butter sandwich yesterday, this would not be an extraordinary claim. You would not have to reject beliefs you already have in order to believe it. If I had said that I had eaten a catfish burger yesterday, this, while less common, would still not fit into the category of the extraordinary. We know that there are catfish and people who eat them. On the other hand, if I had said that I had eaten a unicorn burger, this would be a different matter entirely. To believe that I had eaten part of a unicorn you would have to change some of your beliefs about the reporting of history, the study of zoology, perhaps the methods of exploring the earth, the reliability of news programs that apparently did not widely publicize the discovery of unicorns, or of at least one unicorn, and so on. Before abandoning the reliability of such sources of knowledge, which would call into question much other knowledge that is also dependent upon these methods, you should require a substantial amount of evidence. Enough evidence, at least, to make the supposed fact that I had eaten a unicorn burger much *more* likely than the reliability of zoological reports, news media, and the other relevant sources. The more beliefs you would have to give up, the more evidence you should require. Imagine how much more evidence would be required for you to believe that I had eaten a unicorn burger on a UFO piloted by Elvis! I submit that it would be most rational to *dis*-believe such an account until quite a bit of evidence was presented, or certainly until at least *some* evidence was presented.

b. The claim that god exists is an extraordinary claim.

In the second century C.E., the Christian Tertullian, in his *De Carne Christi* (*On Christ's Flesh*), said of Christianity that "it is certain because it is impossible." He was suggesting that Christianity is to be believed *because* it is so absurd. No one could make up a lie this crazy. Another Christian, Blaise Pascal (1623–1662), famous for his wager, implied that some people may have to take steps to dull their reasoning faculties in order to become Christians. Martin Luther said that reason should be destroyed in all Christians. Thus, it is not simply the atheist's view, but that of many Christians themselves, that belief in god runs counter to reason and common sense. It is an example of an extraordinary claim.

We should, then, demand an extraordinary amount of evidence in favor of theism, or extraordinarily *strong* evidence in its favor, before believing it.

2. Atheism in the absence of evidence is common.

If it did turn out that there is no evidence for the claim that god exists, would it then be *unreasonable* to deny the existence of god? No.

When I have the opportunity, I enjoy confronting theists with a book, written by Michael Jordan (not the sports figure), titled *The Encyclopedia of Gods*.[1] The book contains more than 2,500 of the world's deities. There are, of course, many more in the history of humanity. Every monotheist, such as a Christian, would profess to be *atheistic* about more than 2,499 of those deities. But do these same people profess to know everything before they proclaim that all of these other gods do not exist? Of course not. How many Christians seriously entertain the possibility that the Greek god Zeus, the Roman god Jupiter, or the Norse god Odin actually exist? And what of the gods of Hinduism? Have you ever met someone who has lost sleep wondering whether Titlacahuan, the omnipotent, usually malevolent, Aztec god, really existed? Does any Christian anywhere think that praying to the ancient Armenian god of wisdom named Tir was not an exercise in theological futility? The god Egres of Finland was responsible for the turnip crop, and the god Lactanus made the Roman crops "yield milk" or thrive, yet no Christian believes that these gods ever existed. Is there any Christian who is worried that in the next life he or she may end up in the realm of Tlalchitonatiuh, the Aztec god of the underworld? Of course not. What of all the local gods of volcanos, trees, and rivers who are, and have been, found in other religions around the world? No one has ever been able to "prove" that they do not exist. So are Christians and those of the other major religions agnostic about *them*? They are not. They believe that there are no such gods.

Thus, if there really is no evidence for the existence of a god, it is actually quite *common* to be an atheist regarding that god. This is the view which Christians accept with regard to other gods, so even the Christian accepts this line of reasoning. The only difference between the atheist and the average Christian in this respect is that the atheist does not make an exception for the Christian god. Most theists have a double standard: the criteria for belief in their own gods are different from the standards of evidence to which they hold other gods. The atheist prefers to be consistent and disbelieve in *all* gods until evidence of one or more of them is found.

The claim that god exists is an extraordinary one, and it requires extraordinary evidence in its favor if it is to be believed. In the absence of such evidence it may be considered false. Since there is no strong evidence in favor of this claim, it is rational to conclude that there is no god. The atheist can conclude that god does not exist, and the atheist does not have to know everything in order to do so.

B. The concept of god is incoherent, so god *cannot* exist.

A good case can be made for the notion that the concept of god is incoherent. When I say that the concept of god is incoherent, I do not intend that in a pejorative sense; rather, I mean it quite literally in the sense that the different parts of the concept do not cohere, they do not all fit together conceptually. The concept is self-contradictory. My approach will be twofold. First, I will show that Christians as a group hold incompatible views of god, and then I will show how the traditional Christian concept of god also disagrees with itself, that is, it leads to contradiction and absurdity. My goal in doing this is based on the principle that, although a being with unusual powers or characteristics *may* exist, a being with *contradictory* features *cannot* exist. A contradiction is always, by definition, false.

1. Christians and those of other religions disagree about god's characteristics.

It should come as no surprise to anyone that there are competing views as to the nature of god. Where there is, or has been, monotheism (the view that there is exactly one god), there are, or have been, different accounts of what that being's characteristics are. Christians say one thing, Moslems another, Zoroastrians another, and so on. These claims contradict one another, so they cannot all be true at the same time. Hence, it is impossible for there to exist a being described by all of these religions. A Christian may retort merely that these other religions are false, and that the Christian concept of god is the only correct one, so he or she need not contend with competing views from other religions. This is simply avoiding the issue, but even if it were true, the Christian would not be out of the woods yet. Even among Christians the concept of god is not consistent.

For example, some Christians recognize that if god knows the future, then the future must be already determined, and thus we do not have free will. Others assert that because we do have free will that the future is not fixed, and thus god can know all about the past and the present, but he cannot know the future. Now, god either does or does not know the future, so it cannot be that both of these views are true. Thus, there cannot exist a being who is described by both of these views.

Some Christians believe that their god speaks through an infallible pope. Other Christians deny this. Either there is or there is not a god who speaks through an infallible pope in Rome, so there cannot be a being who is described by both these views.

Some Christians believe in an explicit contradiction—that 1 = 3. I mean, of course, the doctrine of the trinity. Many Christians believe this view in a manner that is explicitly contradictory. In fact, one can even accuse Christianity of not being monotheistic because of the trinity. Of course, other Christians, such as the Jehovah's Witnesses, reject the "one essence, three persons" view, which further compounds the contradictory views within Christianity.

Other examples of contradictory views among Christians are easy to find, so there is no need to dwell on them here. To some

164

extent the different denominations of Christianity are a result of differing interpretations of the concept of god and god's will. Thus, with such a wide range of concepts of god in Christianity, when the atheist is asked whether he or she believes in the Christian god, the atheist may be tempted to reply "Which one?" Where one view is true, another *must* be false. The views cannot possibly all be true at the same time, not simply because they are different, but because they are *contradictory*, so there *cannot* exist a being who matches all of these descriptions. A being who had contradictory attributes could be described correctly by a contradictory statement, but a contradictory statement is defined as one that is necessarily false. A contradiction can never be true in *any* possible circumstances. Thus, there *cannot* exist a being who has contradictory attributes.

2. The concept of a god who possesses the traditional divine attributes reduces to absurdity.

There are some features attributed to god which are inconsistent in all the major versions of theism. Most theists hold that god is omnipotent (all-powerful), omniscient (all-knowing), omnibenevolent (all-good or morally perfect), and transcendent (existing outside of space and time). If it can be shown that a concept of god such as this is incoherent, this would show that the traditional god cannot possibly exist.

There are some obvious contradictions between the traditional god's supposed omniscience and his moral perfection. What is meant by omniscience, or being all-knowing? On some definitions, omniscience is knowing completely everything that can be known. When we speak of knowing, we typically divide knowledge into three categories: 1) factual or propositional knowledge, which is to say that it is expressible as a true sentence or true belief; 2) procedural knowledge, which is the kind of knowledge about how to perform some skill, such as those used in tennis or juggling; and 3) knowledge by personal experience. By this last case we mean roughly that one who says, for example, "I have known poverty" or "I know war" means more than mere belief in the truth of certain sentences. Such a person means that he or she can draw on certain experiences of known circumstances to interpret statements about those circumstances.[2]

Now, could a morally perfect being completely possess all three kinds of knowledge about things in which it is possible to possess such knowledge? Clearly not. For example, Al Capone could know by personal experience what it was like to enjoy running a criminal empire. Surely one important aspect of what it is to enjoy running a criminal empire is the *experience* of doing so. But god, being a morally perfect being, could not know this aspect of running a criminal empire; god cannot enjoy performing evil. Thus Al Capone could know something that an all-knowing being, god, could not. But god is supposed to know everything completely. So the concept is incoherent. Similarly, a serial killer could know by personal experience what it is like to derive pleasure from the torture of his random victims. But god cannot know this, being morally perfect. Thus, a serial killer can know things that an all-knowing being cannot. Again, this is clearly incoherent. God's omnibenevolence is incompatible with his omniscience, so it is impossible for there to exist a being who has both these properties. God is said to have both these properties, so god cannot exist.

It can also be plausibly argued that procedural or skill-knowledge cannot be reduced to statements about beliefs. One can, for example, read all about swimming and practice all the swimming strokes on one's living room couch, but until one has jumped into the water and actually tried swimming, certainly one is missing an important aspect of what it is to swim. Thus, at least part of knowing what it is to perform a skill, such as swimming, would be knowledge which god cannot have because god is outside of space and time. A body takes up space, and god is not in space, since he is transcendent, so god cannot have a body. Since to swim one must be in space and time, and to know completely what it is to swim one must have a body to experience it, god cannot fully know what it is to swim. God's transcendence is incompatible with his omniscience.

At this point some Christians may interject that god had a body in Jesus. However, god is supposed to be omniscient all the time, not just when Jesus was on earth. There is also no record of Jesus ever swimming, although he was supposedly baptized with water, and he was said to have walked on water. Further, there is certainly no record of Jesus ever having the experience of driving a car, drinking soda pop, or experiencing the satisfaction of earning a black belt in karate. These activities were never performed in Jesus' time, so god could not have had experiential knowledge of these things through Jesus. Even if god could know what Jesus experienced, this would not allow god to know all that can be known by experience with a body. God's transcendence is incompatible with his being omniscient all the time, even when Jesus is not using a body, and god's omniscience is not supposed to be intermittent. The concept is incoherent.

Another contradiction of omniscience: I can know what it's like to find out I've made a mistake. Presumably god cannot know this, since it is said that god, who knows all, does not make mistakes, despite the story of the flood. Thus, I am not omniscient, but I can know things an omniscient being cannot. The same can be said of knowing fear, horror, and so on. God is unable to know what it is to have those experiences, but humans can have such knowledge. So the concept of god as an all-knowing being is again contradictory.

There are many other examples of problems of omniscience, but for reasons such as these many Christian philosophers and theologians have abandoned the traditional view of omniscience. However, coming up with another formulation of omniscience that avoids these problems, or others more serious, has thus far eluded theologians.

Contradictions of omnipotence, euphemistically called paradoxes, are well known even to schoolchildren. Can god create a stone too heavy for him or her to lift? If god can do so, then not lifting the stone shows that god is not omnipotent, and, if god cannot create such a stone, then being unable to do so also shows that god is not omnipotent. God either can or cannot create such a stone, but either way god is not omnipotent.

Christian theologians typically respond to these sorts of problems by limiting the definition of god's omnipotence. In fact, some Christians believe that it is logically impossible for god even to *move*, since moving requires time and space, and god does not exist in either. One cannot juggle without moving, so it would be *logically impossible*, by which is meant self-contradictory, for god to do something as simple as juggle or even pick up a pencil. But this contradicts the feature of omnipotence. Surely one would not call all-powerful a being who could not even pick up a pencil. The concept is again incoherent.

God's supposed transcendence results in other serious difficulties. If god exists outside of space and time, then god cannot make a decision. A decision takes place in time. At one moment one is deliberating, and at another moment a decision is made. If there is no time then this process cannot take place. A transcendent god cannot learn, listen, respond to prayer, and perform other such acts. All of those things take place in time. Many theologians have been so unwilling to reject god's transcendence that they have accepted the notion that god cannot change or move in any way. If god does not exist in time, then god cannot perform any action whatsoever. That this means that god could not be active in the world seems not to bother these theologians. They try not to think about it, perhaps.

There are other inconsistent things said about god. God is said to be male, according to the bible, but god cannot be male if god has no body. To possess a body requires space, and god is said to be outside of both space and time. If god does not have a body, then god cannot have genitals. If god does not have genitals, then it is not clear how god could be considered male. God cannot be considered male because of gender orientation because there are presumably no other gods to whom he can be attracted.[3] That god impregnated Jesus' mother Mary (Matt. 1:18, Luke 1:35, and other verses) is inconclusive. The pregnancy was not said to be accomplished physically, otherwise Mary would not be a virgin. That Jesus was male and said to be god is also inconclusive. Surely an omnipotent being could also appear as a woman. God is said to have created man in his image (Gen. 1:26),[4] but god cannot have an image if he, being transcendent, could not have a body. In any case, the next bible verse states that god created man (meaning human beings) in his image, and it states, *"So God created man in his own image, in the image of God he created him; male and female he created them"* (Gen. 1:27 [NIV]). So the alleged image could not have been that of a male if the female also was created in his image. Thus, it makes no sense to consider god a male if god has no body, no image, no genitals, no sexual orientation, and he practices eternal celibacy. The concept of god as a male is inconsistent with his transcendence and other of his features (or lack thereof).

Does god have free will? If god does *not* have free will, then he is by definition unable to perform some actions which it is logically possible to perform. On many definitions of omnipotence, this would mean that god cannot be omnipotent. If god is helpless to change what is going to occur, if his actions are determined, then he is not all-powerful. For example, if it is already determined that god would *not* save a child drowning in Arkansas's White River next Labor Day, then, when that child falls in the river, god would be unable to do anything about it. Most people would not consider a being who could not save a drowning child an omnipotent being, so if god does not have free will, then god is not all-powerful.

However, if god *does* have free will, then god cannot know the future. Knowing the future requires that one know what future states of affairs will occur. If god knows what the future is, then human actions are not free. Some theists can live with that. But if god has free will, then god cannot know what *his own* future actions will be. If he did know, then his actions would be determined in advance and he would not have free will; if god's actions were already determined, if god could not do otherwise than what is predestined, then god would not be free.

If god does not know what his own actions will be, then god cannot know much about the future. For example, if god has free will, he cannot know what human beings will do in the future. Since either god will intervene in the natural course of things and change the outcomes in any given instances or he will not, god cannot know which of these is true in any given instance and still have free will. God could not know, for example, whether he is going to perform a miracle to alter the natural course of events. Suppose that in the ordinary course of nature a large tree that is dead and rotting will, of its own weight, fall on the road in front of a person's car next October 17. This would prevent that person from getting to work on time. If god has free will, then he cannot know whether he will perform a miracle and prevent that tree from falling. If god does not know whether he will intervene, then he cannot know whether the person will get to work on time or any subsequent events which take place because of the person getting to work on time. Thus, if god does not know his own actions in advance, then he cannot know what will happen in the future with regard to human history and other states of affairs.

So, if god is *not* free, then god is not omnipotent, since his will is determined, and if god *is* free, then god is not omniscient, since he will not know the future. God either is or is not free, so he cannot be both omnipotent and omniscient. God is said to be both of these, so god cannot exist.

God's free will may affect his status as a moral being as well. Theories of ethics which are consequentialist are those which use the effects of an act to define its moral status. On a consequentialist moral theory, an act is considered moral if the consequences of the act meet certain criteria, if the act brings about certain results. One may ignore the criteria for the moment so that it may be pointed out that if god cannot know the future because he has free will, then he cannot know the consequences of any given act he performs. If this is so, then god cannot know whether an act he performs is moral, on the consequentialist theory of ethics, because god cannot know the effects of his actions. For example, if a drug-crazed juvenile delinquent is about to shoot some pedestrians on the street, and god inspires a bystander to prevent this, then this would seem to be a moral act. However, if the effects of the act are that it produces more ill effects than good ones, the action may be considered immoral. Suppose that, had the bystander not stopped the gunman, the only pedestrian who would have been shot would have been a mad bomber who, later in the afternoon, kills ten thousand people by setting off some explosives in a crowded stadium. The act of preventing the gunman was immoral, on this view, because it caused such undesirable consequences. Thus, if one is a theist, and one adopts a consequentialist theory of ethics, one must admit that god cannot know with certainty whether any given action he performs is moral. If god has free will, and god cannot know the future, this may conflict with god being all-good.

There are many contradictions to be found in the concept of a god who is said to be omniscient, omnipotent, omnibenevolent, and transcendent. God's gender and his status with regard to free will also conflict with other attributes. Where the concept of a being contradicts itself, the being cannot exist. The traditional concept of god is self-contradictory, so that god cannot exist. The atheist does not have to know everything in order to say that, the atheist just has to know what the theist says about god.

C. The existence of evil is strong evidence against the existence of the traditional god.

The problem of evil should be familiar to almost everyone. In Thomas Hardy's 1878 novel *The Return of the Native*, the character Eustacia Vye exclaims:

> O, the cruelty of putting me into this ill-conceived world! I was capable of much; but I have been injured and blighted and crushed by things beyond my control! O, how hard it is of Heaven to devise such tortures for me, who have done no harm to Heaven at all![5]

This is an expression of a concern which has probably been troubling human beings—at least those who are theists—since prehistoric times. Things happen which cause suffering, and these things could have been prevented by the theistic god, if such a being exists. Why are they not prevented? This is not only a well-known problem for theists, in its stronger formulations it is an effective argument for atheism.[6]

For some believers the problem is easily solved—god is not omnibenevolent. The bible clearly states that god is responsible for evil (Isa. 45:7: *"I form the light, and create darkness: I make peace, and create evil: I the LORD do all these things."* Compare Lam. 3:38 and Amos 3:6). However, most Christians prefer to believe that these parts of the bible are false. Theologians have convinced people to believe, instead, that god is all-good (omnibenevolent). It is this traditional conception of god, that of an omnipotent, omniscient, as well as omnibenevolent being, which is the target of the argument from evil.

1. The existence of evil is incompatible with the existence of the traditional god.

Everyone is aware of events that have happened which we would prefer to have been otherwise. Little babies suffer abuse, people die in earthquakes, and millions die in a famine. These events create human suffering. Let us refer to this suffering as "evil." We all feel intuitively that there are times when, if we could prevent suffering, evil, we would. I would.

Yet theists believe in a being who can presumably prevent *all* suffering, all evil, since the omniscient god knows when suffering is about to occur, and, being all-powerful, has the power to prevent it. And, of course, since he is all-good, it stands to reason that god *would* prevent it. But god does not prevent it. What is the explanation for this? Well, the only possible explanations for this are that god is either unwilling or unable to prevent evil. If god is unwilling to do so, then god is not all-good, and if god is unable to prevent evil, then god is either not all-powerful (he was unable to prevent it even though he may have wanted to do so and knew that

173

this evil would occur), or not omniscient (he did not know that this evil was about to occur), or both. None of these options is agreeable to the theist. Thus, the fact of the existence of evil, or suffering, makes the traditional concept of god untenable.

A good case can be made that the traditional concept of god is the *least likely* hypothesis of all possible explanations for evil. Presumably, we want to look at the evidence for or against god's existence, so we should not *assume* that god exists before we begin the investigation. Facts in the world are surely relevant to our inquiry. One of the facts is that the world contains an awful lot of evil, pain, and suffering, or whatever you want to call it. Now, what is the best explanation for this? If someone *must* offer a theistic explanation, it certainly seems to be most reasonable to describe the cause of something based on features found in its effect. In the supposed effect in question, the world, we find a mix of both good and evil. It would thus seem most reasonable to conclude that whatever produced this world contains both good and evil. However, theists insist that the cause is *un*mixed—god does *not* contain evil— which is the explanation that *least* conforms to features of the world. Thus, of all the possible explanations of the world which contains evil, the explanation that the world was created by a being who is all-good is less plausible than alternative hypotheses, including those which assert that god contains both good and evil, or that there are many gods, some of whom are evil.

Consider this analogy.[7] Imagine that I am shown a series of abstract paintings by an unknown artist, and these are the only paintings the artist is known to have done; it is known that the artist had complete control over what went into making these paintings, and the artist had no help from anyone else. Suppose also that each of the paintings used at least a dozen colors, but at least 40 percent of each painting is in shades of green. Now, if I were asked to speculate regarding this artist's opinion of the color green, it would seem to me to be most reasonable to suggest at least that this artist likes green as well, if not more than, as the other colors, since green is so prominent in the works. Now, you *could* construct some fanciful story about how this artist may actually hate the color green, but the fact that his or her paintings contain so much green makes the hypothesis that this artist likes green, or at least that the artist *doesn't dislike* green, far more believable than the hypothesis that the artist hates green. Of course, the *least* likely hypothesis of all, because it seems clearly false, is that the artist both hates *and* has never, ever owned or even used any green-colored paint at all. Yet it is this last view which the theist would have you accept regarding god, analogous to the painter; the world, analogous to the paintings; and evil, analogous to green. The least likely hypothesis.

If god had no help in making the world, and god had complete control over what went into the world, and god now has the ability to make the world in any way he pleases, and god is omnibenevolent (all-good; that is, he contains no evil), then the world would contain no evil. But it does contain evil. Thus, the view that the theistic god exists and rules the universe is *not* the best explanation for the fact of evil in the world.

If people want to know why evil exists, why it is not prevented, what the theist has to show here is not simply that the god hypothesis is *a possible* explanation, but that it is the *best* explanation for the existence of evil. No one has ever been able to show this. On the contrary, theism is the worst explanation for evil. Thus, the fact of evil in the world makes the theistic view of the world untenable.

2. *Objections to the argument from evil fail.*

There are scores of responses to the argument from evil, which suggests that it is recognized to be a serious problem. Most theologians will readily acknowledge that the argument from evil is extremely damaging to theism. Some of the more popular objections to the argument from evil, and atheists' responses, are given below.

a. *Possible objection: Evil is a punishment for original sin.*

That evil is a punishment for original sin is a common response to the argument from evil. The suggestion is that evil is inherited because of the disobedience of Adam and Eve.

The problem with this explanation, though, is that this supposed defense of god makes god look just as bad, or worse, than he seemed when the argument from evil was intact. Genesis 3:22 and 3:5 have god *and* the serpent, respectively, state explicitly that Adam and Eve did not know the difference between good and evil before eating the magic fruit. In fact, their disobedience consisted in that they *acquired* knowledge of good and evil. Thus, if they did not know the nature of good and evil, they could not possibly have known that disobedience was evil. It is immoral to punish someone for some action that he or she has performed out of ignorance, so the biblical story of Adam and Eve shows god as immoral.

Perhaps an analogy would be useful. Suppose a man were to give an average six-year-old child the following command on the way to dinner: "Dilatory locomotion en route to our repast will incur vehement and unmitigated obloquy and precipitant exoculation." Surely that person would be considered immoral if he later yelled at and blinded the child because the child walked slowly. The child could not have been expected to understand the rule, so any punishment because of its violation was unjust. Similarly, the bible says that Adam and Eve could not have known that disobedience was evil, so they should not be punished for something done out of ignorance.

And what of the nature of the punishment? It certainly seems immoral to punish someone for the disobedience of (supposedly) distant ancestors. Our society would look unfavorably upon someone who went on a rampage killing the children of someone who had offended that person, yet the bible holds that god punishes all people for the actions of two individuals. Parts of the bible seem to agree that punishing someone's offspring is immoral. Deuteronomy 24:16 and Ezekiel 18:19–20 state that children should not suffer for the sins of their parents. Punishing the descendants of someone seems just as incompatible with omnibenevolence as the existence of evil.

In addition, referring to a myth in an ancient book in order to bolster the case for belief in a deity is hardly mustering much support. There is no reason to suppose that the story of the Fall is true, and its mythical characteristics show it to be just another ancient tale about gods. Every culture has them, and there is no reason to suppose that this one is true and the others false.

The Hindus have an account of the creation of women. Before there were women, men were so virtuous that they were easily ascending to divine status and heaven was becoming crowded. Worried, the gods convinced Brahma the creator to create women as a distraction to men and slow them down. According to the story, it worked. There are many other Hindu stories about the origin of evil. Hindus also tell of the many incarnations of the god Vishnu, a god of love and preservation. He comes to help humanity in times of trouble, and they say he has been here nine times, as

Matsya the Fish, Kurma the Tortoise, Varaha the Boar, and other forms. On one occasion, some demons stole the Vedas, the sacred texts, and the creator god Brahma was unable to create. A goddess helped Vishnu recover the Vedas, fortunately.

Some Buddhist sects recount the story that when Siddhartha Gautama, the founder of Buddhism, sat under the bodhi tree to become enlightened, he was tempted and distracted by Mara, the evil one, the tempter, the lord of the world of passion. Gautama prevailed, however, because he was able to draw upon the support of his ten *paramitas*, or great virtues, which he had perfected in previous lives.

The Lakota Indians have a myth in which the four winds, who are brothers, fight over the beautiful woman Wohpe. The South Wind wooed her with beautiful gifts, and she chose to belong to him. This resulted in terrible fights among the four brothers, disputes which last to this day.

Are these stories any less plausible than some told in the bible? Can anyone read of the wager between god and the devil in Job, or the story of Jacob whipping god in a wrestling match (Gen. 32:22–32) without realizing that the biblical myths are no different in kind?[8]

The appeal to the story of Adam and Eve as a defense to the problem of evil fails.

b. Possible objection: Evil is necessary so that we can have knowledge of good.

Some theists argue that it is only through suffering evil that one can learn what is good. But you don't need to have your hands cut off in order to know that it is undesirable. You don't need to be lost at sea in order to know the value of a map. God must not be too bright, on this view, if he can't think of any way to impart knowledge of good other than to slaughter billions of people throughout human history. If god is omnipotent, why can't he just put the idea of good into our heads without killing someone? Why couldn't god instead produce an overwhelming amount of good to give us the idea of evil, instead of the other way around? This response fails.

c. Possible objection: Free will causes evil.

The free will defense is that god gives people the free will to act as they choose, and it is people, not god, who cause evil. The free will of people cannot be controlled by god because then it would not be free. God gave people free will because it is so valuable that its good outweighs any evil that people might perform. This response is of limited value.

(i) If humans have free will, then god does not know the future.

Those who wish to use the free will defense must, in most cases, abandon the claim that god knows the future. Not all theists are willing to do that. If god knew the future, then the future would be determined in advance, and humans could not choose otherwise than they do. Some philosophers, called *compatibilists*, attempt to show that free will and determinism are somehow true at the same time, but other philosophers have not found their arguments to be persuasive. The concept of human free will undermines claims about god's omniscience.

179

(ii) It is not clear that the goodness of free will could justify all evil.

Even if it were granted (which it is not) that free will causes all the suffering in the world, could the supposed goodness of free will be so good as to justify god allowing all the suffering that occurs? Theologians often claim that god has given human beings free will despite the supposed fact that humans abuse it by choosing to do evil. Some theologians hold that god knew well in advance that the privilege of free will would be used to fill the world with evil, but he chose to give humans free will anyway, because free will is such a good in itself that it outweighs the amount of evil in the world. Could the world be so much better because we are free that it doesn't matter whether people suffer? The theologian Eugene Borowitz wrote:

> Any God who could permit the Holocaust, who could remain silent during it, who could "hide His face" while it dragged on, was not worth believing in. There might well be a limit to how much we could understand about Him, but Auschwitz demanded an unreasonable suspension of understanding. In the face of such great evil, God, the good and the powerful, was too inexplicable, so men said "God is dead."[9]

Human history, unfortunately, is filled with many other examples of suffering. The torture and abuse of children is such an atrocity it seems unlikely that the supposed fact of free will could be so good as to justify it.

(ii) The free will defense does not explain natural evil.

Philosophers and theologians often distinguish between *moral evil* and *natural evil*. Moral evil is suffering caused by the supposedly free actions of human beings. Natural evil is suffering caused by events unrelated to free, intentional human action. Natural disasters and unintentional human error are examples of natural evil. The free will defense to the problem of evil does not address the issue of natural evil.

From 1347 to 1351, several plagues known collectively as the Black Death killed over 75 million people in Eurasia. In a nine-month period in 1918, over 21 million people worldwide died of influenza. This is more than twice the number of those who died in the First World War. A famine in China from 1969 to 1971 killed 20 million people. A monsoon in the Ganges Delta isles of Bangladesh killed a million people on November 12–13, 1970. An earthquake in the Shensi province of China killed 830,000 people on January 23, 1556. The 1883 eruption of the Indonesian volcano Krakatoa killed 36,000 people, most of them with a tidal wave. Italy's volcanic Mount Etna, in 1669, killed 20,000. A tidal wave in Awa, Japan, in 1703, killed more than 100,000 people. An avalanche of snow in Peru killed over 18,000 people on May 31, 1970.

A compassionate person would feel compelled to prevent such suffering if given the opportunity, and an omniscient and omnipotent god has unlimited opportunity. God is not off the hook even if it is granted that free will does cause some suffering. Millions die in agony from natural evil and god does nothing. The free will defense is silent on that.

The free will defense undermines god's omniscience. It does not explain the vast amount of evil in the world, and it does not address the existence of natural evil at all. This defense fails.

d. Possible objection: Satan causes evil.

God is the author of evil, according to Isaiah 45:7, Lamentations 3:38, and other biblical verses. However, many Christians attempt to place the blame on Old Scratch—the devil. To do so, however, the Christian must abandon the claim of god's omnipotence. If god is all-powerful, then no one can do anything which god cannot prevent. In other words, if god is all-powerful, then god can prevent evil no matter who is trying to perform it. In effect, this makes god an accomplice to all evil. If the Christian wants to maintain that god is omnipotent, not even Satan can save god from the argument from evil.

e. Possible objection: God has an unknown but morally sufficient reason for not preventing evil.

Some theists admit that they have no explanation for the fact that god allows evil, but they assert that we know that he must have a good enough reason, a morally sufficient reason, for not preventing evil because we know that god is omnibenevolent. Since an omnibenevolent being would not allow evil without a sufficiently strong reason, we know that god must have such a reason.

This objection to the argument from evil is easily overcome.

i. The claim is a mere assertion.

The claim that god has a secret, morally sufficient reason for not preventing evil is not supported by any evidence. There is no empirical support for this claim. No experience justifies the assertion that god has a secret reason for permitting evil. Without evidence in its favor, there is no reason to believe that it is true. If there is no reason to believe that the claim is true, then there is no reason to believe that this objection to the argument from evil is successful. The existence of evil, the evidence which is to be explained, is at least *prima facie* evidence that there is not an omibenevolent god. Thus, there is no reason to believe that this claim, that god has a morally sufficient reason to permit evil, is true, and at least some reason to believe that it is false, so this objection to the argument from evil fails.

ii. The claim begs the question at issue.

The claim that god must have a morally sufficient reason for not preventing evil because he is omnibenevolent begs the question. The issue is whether there is a god who is, among other things, omnibenevolent. The argument from evil is the presentation of the evidence of evil in the world, and the fact of evil counts as evidence against the existence of the theistic god. Given the evidence, we can conclude that a being such as god does not exist. The suggestion that we know that god has a good reason for not preventing evil *because* he is all-good assumes exactly what the evidence speaks against—that there is an all-good god. To state that we can conclude something *from the fact that god is omnibenevolent* already assumes that there is a god who is omnibenevolent. In order for this move to be successful it must *first* be shown that there is a god who is omnibenevolent. If this can be established, then the theist can explain what follows from this fact. That fact has not been established, unlike the fact that human suffering exists, so this objection to the argument from evil fails. The most that such an approach would be able to establish would be that *if* the theistic god did exist *and* evil existed also, *then* we could conclude that god would have a morally sufficient reason for permitting evil. Until the existence of the theistic god has been shown, however, no conclusions can be drawn from the supposed fact of his existence.

iii. The inability to produce the reason that god permits evil makes the existence of god unlikely.

The lack of a successful explanation for evil decreases the probability that god exists. After all, as the theist claims, if god were to exist, then there would be a morally sufficient reason for him to permit evil. If it is unlikely that there is a morally sufficient reason for evil, then it is unlikely that god exists. The more theists are unable to produce the morally sufficient reason, the more likely it is that there isn't one, and the more likely it is that god does not exist.

Consider the painter analogy again. Suppose that a Ms. Pigment were to maintain that the painter whose works show a high percentage of green really detests green, will have nothing to do with green, and discourages the use of green by others. Since the evidence is at odds with her claim, the burden is on Ms. Pigment to produce an explanation for the occurrence of green in this artists's paintings. If she cannot produce the reason, then we are justified in concluding that her claim is false, since the evidence suggests otherwise.

Similarly, if someone maintains that there is an all-powerful, all-knowing god who hates evil, the burden is on that person to explain the existence of evil. If no reason is given, or if the reason is called a "secret," which is the same as not giving a reason, then we are justified in concluding that the claim is false.

The "secret reason" defense fails.

The argument from evil is strong evidence against the existence of the traditional god. Those who believe in a god who is evil, or who is at least partly evil, would be unaffected by the argument from evil. Similarly, those who believe in more than one god, at least one of whom is evil and equal in power to good gods, would not be affected by this argument. Traditional theists, however, cannot ignore this powerful argument against the existence of their god.

D. The existence of nonbelievers is evidence that god does not exist.

Those who believe that there is a god who is omnipotent, omniscient, and omnibenevolent must explain the fact that their god does not reveal himself convincingly to everyone. Many devout theists have grappled with this issue. St. Anselm (1034–1109) wrote: "If thou art everywhere, why do I not see thee present?"[10] And Pascal: "God being thus hidden, any religion that does not say that God is hidden is not true, and any religion which does not explain why does not instruct."[11] If god exists, then, why does god not reveal himself to all?

For some theists, the explanation is simple: the bible makes it clear in a number of passages that *god does not want everyone to be saved.* For example, Isaiah 6:9–13 has Isaiah commissioned by god to go make sure that certain people do not hear or understand, so that they will surely be destroyed. Quoting one of these passages from Isaiah, Jesus also made it plain that he speaks in parables because he does not want everyone to understand his teaching and be saved (Mark 4:10–12, Matt. 13:11–15). John 12:40 also cites a passage from Isaiah to explain that god has made some

185

people unable to turn and be healed. Second Thessalonians 2:11–12 explains that, with regard to some people, god will *"send them strong delusion, that they should believe a lie: That all might be damned who believed not the truth. . . ."* In addition, many people, according to the bible, are not to be told about god's message for salvation. Jesus initially ignored a Gentile's pleas for help and said that he was here for the "lost sheep of the house of Israel" (Mark 7:26–27, Matt. 15:22–26). He commanded his disciples, when sending them forth, to avoid the Gentiles and not to enter any city of the Samaritans (Matt. 10:5).[12] The holy spirit kept Paul and his companions from preaching in Asia (Acts 16:6),[13] and "the spirit of Jesus" (NIV) kept them from preaching in Bithynia (Acts 16:7). Second John 9–10 forbids simply *greeting* nonbelievers; anyone who greets, *"wishes God speed,"* to a nonbeliever *"is a partaker of his evil deeds."* How anyone is supposed to be converted when he or she cannot even be greeted is not explained.

Thus, by divine intervention to confuse or deceive people, by intentionally withholding the meanings of parables, or by simply not allowing everyone to hear the supposed "good news," the god of the bible seems to ensure that large numbers of people, if not the majority of humanity, will roast in hell for eternity.

Many Christians find the idea of god causing people to be sent to hell, of god not wanting everyone to be saved, distasteful. They prefer to ignore the passages of the bible which support such a view and believe the few conflicting verses which suggest that god does want everyone to be saved. Bible passages such as 1 Timothy 2:3–4 (*"God our Saviour, who will have all men to be saved, and to come unto the knowledge of the truth"*) and 2 Peter 3:9 (*"The Lord is . . . not willing that any should perish"*), present a more pleasant view of god. It is this conception of god, that of a being who is omnipotent, omniscient, and omnibenevolent, who wants everyone to be saved, which is subjected to attack in the argument from nonbelief.

186

1. The existence of nonbelievers is incompatible with the existence of the traditional god.

Many freethinkers throughout history have asked the theists to explain why it is that god does not cause his message to be heard by more people. Surely part of what it is to love someone is to want that person to have good fortune and avoid tragedy. Wishing that the person go to heaven (if there were one) and avoid eternal agony in hell (if there were such a place) would be examples of expressing love. If people are in danger of hellfire, and they have a chance to avoid it, why doesn't the good god see to it that everyone believes what is necessary to be saved?

a. The argument from nonbelief uses the traditional concept of god.

The philosopher Theodore Drange, of West Virginia University, is the originator of the argument from nonbelief. He has taken some intuitions about god and salvation, which other critics of theism have had, and created a powerful argument against the existence of god. In *Evil and Nonbelief: Two Arguments for the Nonexistence of God*, he formulates the argument in a manner similar to the following, simplified version.[14]

First, let set P be defined as the set of the following three propositions: (a) There exists a being who is omnipotent, omniscient, and omnibenevolent; (b) This being loves humanity; and (c) This being wants each person to be saved. Let us assume for the sake of simplicity that anyone who believes the propositions in set P is saved, and anyone who does not believe them is punished. One may add to set P additional propositions such as "Jesus died

187

for your sins," "Jesus rose from the dead," or similar propositions without affecting the argument. With this definition of P, the argument can be formulated.

b. The argument from nonbelief concludes that the traditional god cannot exist.

The argument from nonbelief is the following:

1. If god were to exist, then god would be able to convince everyone that the propositions in set P are true.

God, being omnipotent, could plant the ideas in people's heads, cause the propositions to appear floating in the air over major cities, change all the sentences of this book into the propositions of P, and so on. No one need remain ignorant, or unconvinced, of the propositions of set P. God could present them miraculously, if that's what it takes to make them convincing.

2. If god were to exist, god would *want* everyone to be saved.

If god were truly omnibenevolent, if god really loved everyone, then he would want what is best for everyone. Obviously, being saved is what is best for everyone.

3. If god were to exist, god would not want anything more than he wants to have everyone saved (since he loves humanity).

For example, god would not want people to be damned more than he would want them to be saved.

4. Given (1)–(3), if god were to exist, then everyone would believe the propositions in set P.
5. Not everyone believes the propositions in P. Not everyone is saved.

---

6. Therefore, god does not exist.

In other words, if god did exist, he would want everyone to be saved. If people are saved by believing certain things, then god would see to it that everyone would have those beliefs. But not everyone has those beliefs. Thus, god does not exist.

Consider this analogy. Suppose that a person, Mr. Rescue, has four children. One fateful day the four children are trapped in the top floor of their house, which is on fire. The room in which they find themselves has a fire escape, but it is behind a locked door. To open the door they must punch in a series of four numbers on the door's combination lock (a design flaw, obviously). If they do this, they can easily exit and save themselves. Unfortunately, they do not know the combination to the lock. However, Mr. Rescue arrives on the scene and sees that his children are trapped in the house, and he knows the combination which can save them. He also has a cellular telephone, and there is a telephone in the room with the children. Mr. Rescue can simply call the children and tell them the four numbers to the combination lock. Mr. Rescue claims that he loves his children and wants them to be saved. Should he make the call? The answer seems obvious.

If god does exist, then why doesn't god see to it that we, like the children in the house, get the information that we need in order to be saved? Not just get the information, but *believe* the information. If god exists, and god is all-powerful and all-knowing, then god could see to it that the information needed to save each person, the beliefs in set P, are presented in such a way as to be universally believed. This has not happened. This shows that god does not exist.

2. Objections to the argument from nonbelief fail.

There are a number of possible objections to the argument from nonbelief. Because the argument, at least in this form, has so recently been introduced to the field of the philosophy of religion, it is not clear which objections will be the most favored among theists. However, it is not difficult to anticipate some of the most likely objections.[15]

a. Possible objection: The bible is sufficient evidence to convince people of the propositions of P.

Some Christians might object to the argument from nonbelief with the claim that god *has* made the propositions in set P sufficiently clear so that every person should believe them, and god has done this through his word in the bible. God wants everyone to read or hear the bible and be saved.

i. The bible is not universally convincing.

Previous observations about the bible should suffice to refute objections which rely on the bible as evidence of god's supposed desire to have everyone saved. Leaving something as important as salvation to a book which is known to contain forgery, contradiction, and other kinds of falsehoods is hardly showing love for those whose lives (or supposed souls) depend on that information. If god wants everyone to be saved by reading the bible, then the bible ought to be extremely convincing. But it is not.

H. L. Mencken said: "What I got in Sunday School . . . was simply a firm conviction that the Christian faith was full of palpable absurdities, and the Christian God preposterous."[16] Mencken's comment echoes what many have discovered: it is often *the study of the bible* which leads one to conclude that its claims are false!

Thomas Paine observed: "All the tales of miracles with which the Old and New Testament are filled, are fit only for impostors to preach and fools to believe."[17] Paine read the bible carefully, thoughtfully, and conscientiously—and concluded that there is overwhelming evidence that the absurd stories in the bible are false.

W. S. Ross (1844–1909), a freethinker and book publisher, studied for the ministry and, as a result, became an atheist. He wrote:

> Jack and his beanstalk was just as suitable for the nucleus of a religious system as Christ and his cross; but the one has been taken and the other left. Christ and his cross is the more blood-stained and crude legend of the two, and would, therefore, receive the readier acceptance by the barbarous mental and moral instincts of priest-manipulated ignorance.[18]

Ross is only one of many who have become atheists *by reading the bible.*

Farrell Till was a minister, missionary to France, and pious member of the Church of Christ. After studying at more than one seminary, and then beginning his ministry, he made the time to study the bible in more depth than he had previously. This caused him to abandon Christianity. He now edits *The Skeptical Review*, a newsletter about bible errancy. He is quite candid about the fact that it was the bible which made him an atheist.

A. A. Milne, the creator of Winnie the Pooh, is said to have commented:

> The Old Testament is responsible for more atheism, agnosticism, disbelief—call it what you will—than any [other] book ever written; it has emptied more churches than all the counterattractions of cinema, motor-bicycling and golf course.[19]

Such reactions to the bible are not uncommon. If thousands of men and women of intelligence and good conscience can examine the bible and concur that it is a lot of nonsense, then the Christian must admit that the bible is *not* sufficiently convincing to bring about belief in the propositions of set P in every person. In fact, there are many cases in which the absurd claims of the bible have caused people to abandon belief in god. If there were a god who really did want everyone to be saved by reading the bible, surely god would have seen to it that the bible would have been much more convincing than it is at present. Indeed, the bible is so unconvincing that it cannot even withstand the most superficial investigation into its reliability, let alone a thorough one—so god does not exist.

ii. The bible could have shown signs of divine origin, but it does not.

If the bible really were the word of an omnipotent, omniscient being, and this being wanted everyone to know that this book has an origin unlike any other in history, namely, that it has a divine source, this could have been easily accomplished. The bible could have had a well-documented history. It needn't have been mostly anonymous, as it is now. It could have had stories which are unique, instead of those which it presently has, which were common among superstitious people when the bible was written. The bible could have been inerrant instead of a mass of contradiction, error, and absurdity. The bible could have reflected omniscience by explaining scientific theories which it would have been impossible for humans to know in primitive times. Instead, it reflects errors in science and cosmology which were typical among ancient cultures. Finally, the bible itself could have been accompanied by a miracle. Thomas Paine explains:

> Something . . . was necessary *as a miracle*, to have proved that what [Jesus] delivered was the word of God; and this was that the book in which that word should be contained, which is now called the Old and New Testament, should possess the miraculous property, distinct from all human books, of resisting alteration. This would be not only a miracle, but an ever existing and universal miracle . . . [and] would prove, in all ages and in all places, the book to be divine and not human. . . .[20]

The bible could have been miraculously resistant to alteration and forgery. Instead, the bible's history contains extensive alteration and forgery.

iii. The bible has not been available to everyone.

If there were a god who wanted everyone to be saved, and the recipe for salvation were contained in a book, then one would expect that the book would be available to everyone. But most of the humans who have existed on this planet have never seen or heard of the Christian bible. Why did god not cause bibles to rain from the sky? Why haven't bibles been in every home throughout history? A god who wants everyone to be saved would let everyone know how this is to be accomplished. This has not been done, so this shows that there is no such god.

iv. There are sacred books of other religions.

If there were a god whose plans of salvation were in one book, and that god wanted everyone to be saved, then that god would not allow false books to fill the world. But there are millions of copies of the *Tao Te Ching*, the *Bhagavad-Gita*, the *Koran*, and other holy books. Modern-day gurus such as Deepak Chopra and James Redfield sell New Age "spiritual" books by the millions. A god who really wants his plan of salvation followed would not allow other plans to be promulgated. The more false plans available, the more likely it is that someone will believe a false plan for salvation. If there were a god who wants everyone to be saved, he would make it unlikely for people to encounter and believe false plans for salvation. But the theist admits that there are countless other plans, all of them false, with millions of followers. Thus, there is no such god.

Clearly, the bible is insufficient to instill belief in everyone. An omniscient and omnipotent being could have done far better had he decided to become an author. Even if the theist were to insist that somehow, in some way, at some unspecified time in the future, some theologians will show that there is solid, historical evidence that the stories in the bible are true (which is just the opposite of what is currently the case), the theist must still explain why the bible is *currently* so unconvincing. Why would god, who presumably wants all people to be saved, put the means of salvation in a book which, even in the event of its later exoneration, at present *so closely resembles a pack of lies?* One would *at least* expect that god would provide a book that would not be so absurd that it would cause people to become atheists! The appeal to the bible as a defense fails.

b. Possible objection: Nature is available to all. It is sufficient evidence.

Some theists argue that the existence of nature is proof of the existence of god. Others hold that some facts about nature, such as its design, show that god exists. This is how god makes himself known and shows us "the way."

i. Arguments for the existence of god based on nature have failed.

Those who think that nature is proof of god's existence are mistaken, as explained elsewhere in this book.[21] The existence of nature shows nothing about gods.

ii. The existence of nature is compatible with many views about gods.

The existence of nature is compatible with atheism (the view that there are no gods), monotheism (the view that there is exactly one god), polytheism (the view that there are many gods), pantheism (the view that god *is* the universe or nature), panpsychism (the view that everything has a soul),[22] and many other beliefs related to gods. After all, those who believe each of those systems agree that the universe exists. If the existence of the universe does not conflict with any of those systems, its existence cannot count as evidence for one of those views and not the others. Thus, the existence of the universe or nature cannot show that any given god or set of gods exists, and *ipso facto* cannot show any particular god's plan for salvation.

iii. The existence of nature does not contain a message of salvation.

The existence of nature is not evidence of a god or gods, so nature certainly cannot be evidence of any particular plan of salvation. There is no message of love, salvation, damnation, or anything else evident in nature. In the words of French novelist Anatole France (1844–1924):

> Nature has no principles. She furnishes us with no reason to believe that human life is to be respected. Nature, in her indifference, makes no distinction between good and evil.[23]

The existence of nature furnishes no clue as to the disposition of any god, whether it is good or evil, loving or indifferent. If there were a god who wanted everyone to be saved, and nature were the means to convey the message of salvation, then nature would show clear and unequivocal evidence of that message. But there is no such message in nature. Thus, there is no such god.

c. Possible objection: God wants people to believe through free will.

Another possible objection to the argument from nonbelief is that there is a god who wants human beings to be saved, but he wants even more that they exercise their free will. Thus, god does not want to force human beings to believe in him. Instead, he wants humankind to come to know and love him freely. This is an attempt to undermine premise (3) of the argument from nonbelief.

The obvious problem with this objection is that having free will is *compatible* with being thoroughly convinced that god exists and wants us to be saved. If there were a god who wanted us to know the propositions in set P, god could see to it that everyone encountered overwhelming evidence to that effect, and each person would still be in a position to freely use his or her judgment to come to the decision that the propositions of set P are true. Just as each reader of this sentence retained his or her free will when taught to read and write, each could have been taught *with evidence* that god exists, loves humanity, and wants each of us to be saved. A person's free will would not be compromised by this. Since free will and convincing everyone of the propositions of P are compatible, this defense fails.

d. Possible objection: God wants people to believe through faith.

Some theists might claim that god wants everyone to be saved, but he does not want to provide evidence. He wants everyone to believe without evidence; he desires each person to come to believe the propositions of set P through faith.

There are many problems with belief on the basis of faith, as I will show later. The main problem with regard to salvation, however, is that simply wanting people to believe certain propositions, without providing convincing evidence that the propositions are true, is an extremely unreliable method of getting people to adopt a particular set of beliefs. Because there are many other religions competing for belief, providing no evidence for the "true" religion makes it unlikely that everyone will choose the (supposedly) correct one. Thus, at least some portion of the population is guaranteed damnation. That is incompatible with omnibenevolence.

A return to our analogy of the burning house may be useful. Suppose that Mr. Rescue had written the combination to the lock on the wall of the room in which the children are trapped. However, there are thousands of other four-digit combinations, which are *incorrect,* also written on the walls of that same room. Mr. Rescue refuses to tell the children in the house which combination is the one that opens the door. Instead, he wants them to try to guess it correctly by choosing one from the many written on the walls. Could it be said that Mr. Rescue really loves his children? Does it seem that he really wants them to be saved? Hardly.

Similarly, if there were a god who wanted everyone to follow some plan for salvation, the truth of this plan would be easily distinguishable from the thousands of false plans of other religions. But the plan, if there is one, is *in*distinguishable from any of the others with regard to its truth. There are dozens of other major religions in the world today, there are thousands of smaller religions and cults, and there have been tens of thousands of others in the history of humanity. Christianity is just another religion with a host of grand promises, scary threats, and *no* evidence. If there were a god who wanted everyone to adopt Christianity, then this god would have made sure that Christianity—or whatever other religion is the intended one—could show that its claims are true. Christianity cannot do this. Nor can any other religion. Thus, there is no god who sincerely wants everyone to follow his plan for salvation.

e. Possible objection: God is testing everyone.

Theists may object to the argument from nonbelief with the claim that god is testing everyone. God wants to see who believes the propositions in set P given the amount of evidence now available.

Since there is no evidence for the propositions of set P, however, the claim that god is testing everyone undermines god's supposed omnibenevolence. A good god would not conduct a test to see whether some people would make a certain choice based on *no* evidence when that person's eternal fate depends upon the outcome. If there is no evidence for the propositions of set P, then there is no reason to expect someone to believe those propositions, and this objection becomes the same as the objection on the grounds that god wants people to be saved through faith. A test to see who will believe a set of extraordinary propositions for no reason is not a test for moral character, and certainly not for intelligence. What is being tested, if not gullibility or ignorance? And why would a just god want only the most gullible and ignorant to be saved?

Some theists assert that there *is* sufficient evidence for the propositions of P, and that god is testing everyone to see who will realize that the evidence proves the truth of the claims of theism. This assertion is easily dismissed. For example, most people have never even heard of the propositions of P with respect to a particular god, especially the Christian god, so these people have never even had the opportunity to reject Christianity. The test would be grossly unfair if most human beings have flunked the test without even being given a chance to take it! A god who really wants everyone to be saved would make sure that everyone has a chance to look at the evidence. This has not happened, however. I have never seen *any* evidence, and billions of other people have lived and died and have seen no evidence.

To support this objection to the argument from nonbelief, the burden is on the theist to show that there is sufficient evidence for the propositions of P, and no theist has been able to demonstrate this.

Besides, if god is all-knowing, why would he need to conduct a test?

f. Possible objection: God has a secret reason for not convincing everyone of the truth of the propositions of set P.

A theist may, in desperation, assert that god has a secret reason, an unknown purpose, for not bringing it about that everyone holds the beliefs in set P. To this there are two obvious responses.

i. There is no reason to believe that there is an unknown purpose.

If there is no reason to believe that god has a secret motive for not convincing everyone of the propositions of P, the claim is a mere assertion with no weight whatsoever. If there is no reason to believe that god has an unknown purpose, this cannot be a legitimate reason to reject the argument from nonbelief. One who appeals to the unknown purpose objection is really saying nothing other than: "Although I cannot explain how it is so, it could be possible that the argument from nonbelief fails, for some reason." It is conceded that it may fail for some reason, but unless there is some evidence that it *does* fail, the argument achieves its objective; it shows that theism is untenable. Until there is some reason to believe that there is a flaw in the argument from nonbelief, simply pointing out that there *might* be one, via some unknown purpose in the mind of god, accomplishes nothing.

ii. The unknown purpose undermines at least one of god's attributes.

If there is a god who does not take the steps necessary to bring about widespread belief in P, then this suggests that god is either not omnibenevolent or not omniscient or not omnipotent. In other

200

words, regardless of the reason, whether it is known or unknown, either god does not *want* to bring about universal belief in the propositions of P, in which case god is not all-good; god does not *know how* to bring about universal acceptance of those beliefs, in which case god is not all-knowing, or god is *unable* to bring about that situation, in which case god is not all-powerful. Since god is said to possess all three of those properties, the unknown purpose objection actually denies that there is such a god. Hence, this objection fails.

g. Possible objection: Satan causes unbelief.

Some theists would blame the devil for unbelief. God wants everyone to be saved, but the malicious actions of Satan cause some to be nonbelievers.

i. An appeal to the bible regarding Satan's activities is ineffective.

Satan does very little in the bible, and he is never even depicted as lying, at least not without explicit orders from god to do so (such as 1 Kings 22:20–23 and 2 Chron. 18:19–22, if the lying spirit is Satan). Passages in the bible, such as John 8:44, call the devil a liar and the father of lies, but the bible does not contain any examples of the devil lying in order to cause unbelief. Second Corinthians 4:4 states that *"the god of this age hath blinded the minds of them which believe not, lest the light of the glorious gospel of Christ, who is the image of God, should shine unto them."* It is assumed by many that the god mentioned in this verse is Satan, but it is not clear that this is interpretation is correct. In any case, as noted earlier, the god of the bible—the main one, not any of the other ones it mentions—causes unbelief too (2 Thess. 2:11). Can

201

nonarbitrary grounds be given for rejecting the verses about god causing unbelief and yet not rejecting those which state that Satan causes unbelief? It seems unlikely. Those who wish to appeal to the vague verses which *may* show that Satan causes unbelief must confront the *explicit* passages which state the same of god.

But if god causes unbelief, too, this would undermine the attribute of omnibenevolence; it would, in effect, be an acknowledgement that the god of theism, who is omnibenevolent, does not exist. But this is exactly what the argument from nonbelief is designed to establish! The appeal to the bible backfires on the theist. This defense fails.

ii. There is no nonbiblical evidence that Satan causes unbelief.

The claim that Satan causes people to be unbelievers must be supported by evidence if it is to be an effective objection to the argument from nonbelief. Unfortunately, there is no evidence that devils exist. Mental illness, depression, epilepsy, and other afflictions which used to be attributed to demons are now known to have natural causes. Further, because there are sound, plausible arguments to show that god does not exist, there are good reasons to believe that nonbelief is caused by conscientious thinking, by rational principles, and not by devils. This objection does not work.

iii. The Satan objection undermines god's omnipotence.

Those who assert that Satan causes unbelief while god wishes for everyone to be a believer seem to forget that god is supposed to be more powerful than Satan. If Satan can bring about circumstances which are contrary to god's will, this suggests that god is not all-powerful. As we saw earlier with the Satan objection to the argument from evil, those who claim that Satan can defy god admit that their god is not all-powerful and thus admit that the traditional god does not exist. Again, since this is also the conclusion of the argument from nonbelief, this supposed defense is really an admission of defeat.

If there were a god who is omnipotent, omniscient, and omnibenevolent, that being would want everyone to be saved. If salvation depends on holding certain beliefs, such a god would and could see to it that everyone holds those beliefs. But this has not happened. Thus, there is no such god.

Conclusion

A.   Atheism in the absence of evidence is an accepted principle.
B.   The concept of god is incoherent, so god *cannot* exist.
C.   The existence of evil is strong evidence against the traditional god.
D.   The existence of nonbelievers is evidence that god does not exist.

Therefore, the claim that atheists must know everything in order to claim that god does not exist is groundless.

Theists who claim that atheism requires omniscience are thus confronted with several responses, each of which is sufficient to show that atheism is justified despite the fact that human knowledge is finite. The first argument shows that the atheist can rationally, in accordance with common sense, conclude that there is no god given the lack of evidence in favor of theism. The second argument shows that the existence of the traditional god is *impossible* because the concept of the being said to exist is contradictory. The last two arguments show that there are empirical facts of the world—evil and nonbelief—which make theism untenable. Omniscience is not required.

Of the four arguments above, the first, perhaps, provides the atheist with the most opportunities for amusement. Upon hearing that I am an atheist, theists sometimes extend a palm and exclaim: "Really? You're an atheist? Well, I want to shake your hand! If you know that god does not exist you must be the smartest person in the world!"

To which I respond: "Oh, so you think a god exists? Do you believe that Odin exists?"

The theists invariably (so far) respond, "No."

"Do you believe that Zeus exists?" Again a negative answer.

"How about the Roman god Jupiter? No?"

At this point the theist usually informs me of his or her theological preference.

"Well, do you mean to tell me that of the tens of thousands of gods that people have believed in throughout history, you are an atheist about all but one of them? Atheism about only *one* god separates you and me? Well, even if I am the smartest person in the world, you should not be so impressed. *You must rate a close second!*"

Notes

1. Michael Jordan, *The Encyclopedia of the Gods: Over 2,500 Deities of the World* (New York: Facts on File, 1993). The information about non-Christian gods in the remainder of the paragraph is from this work.

2. See Michael Martin, *Atheism: A Philosophical Justification* (Philadelphia: Temple University Books, 1990), p. 287. Chapter 12 of Martin's book is an excellent exposition of the incoherence of the concept of god.

3. Some Israelite traditions did give god some companionship, however. Asherah, mentioned in verses such as 2 Kings 18:4, was a Canaanite mother goddess said to be god's consort.

4. The bible actually says *"our image"* using the plural. Of course, Genesis contains more than one creation story. The story from Genesis chapter 2, for example, differs from that of the first chapter.

5. Thomas Hardy, *The Return of the Native* (New York: Simon & Schuster, 1972), p. 404.

6. It is thought that the ancient Greek philosopher Epicurus (341–270 B.C.E.) first formulated the problem of evil.

7. Cf. Nelson Pike's "Hume on Evil," in *The Problem of Evil*, Marilyn McCord Adams and Robert Merrihew Adams, eds. (New York: Oxford University Press, 1990), pp. 38–51.

8. The Hindus' Matsya the Fish, an incarnation of Vishnu, helped a fellow named Manu build a boat so that Manu could survive a catastrophic flood. The Babylonian Epic of Gilgamesh, based on an even older seventeenth-century version, also tells a flood story similar to that of Noah, even down to the releasing of birds so that they can find signs of vegetation. Scholars believe that the Noah version is either based on the Babylonian account or both are derived from an even older flood story.

9. Eugene Borowitz, *The Mask Jews Wear* (New York: Simon & Schuster, 1973), p. 99.

10. St. Anselm, *Proslogion*, in *St. Anselm: Basic Writings*, S. N. Deane, trans., 2d ed. (LaSalle, Ill.: Open Court, 1968), p. 3.

11. Blaise Pascal, *Pensées*, A. Krailsheimer, trans. (New York: Penguin Books, 1966), section 424.

12. Oddly, Peter was an apostle to the Gentiles anyway and stated that god *encouraged* preaching to the Gentiles (Acts 15:7).

13. Paul, like Peter, ignored the divine moratorium and preached in Asia anyway (Acts 19:8–10).

14. Theodore Drange, *Nonbelief and Evil: Two Arguments for the Nonexistence of God* (Amherst, N.Y.: Prometheus Books, 1998). See also "The Argument from Nonbelief," *Religious Studies* 29 (1993): 417–32.

15. Objections "c," "e," and "f," especially, are anticipated in Drange's work.

16. Quoted in *The Portable Curmudgeon*, Jon Winokur, ed. (New York: Penguin Books, 1992), p. 66.

17. Thomas Paine, "Extract from a Reply to the Bishop of Llandaff," from *A Second Anthology of Atheism and Rationalism*, Gordon Stein, ed. (Amherst, N.Y.: Prometheus Books, 1987), p. 158. This anthology will be called "Stein 2" hereafter.

18. W. S. Ross, "Did Jesus Christ Rise from the Dead?" (1887), reprinted in Stein, p. 206. Ross wrote under the pen name "Saladin."

19. Attributed to Milne in *Whatever It Is, I'm against It*, Nat Shapiro, ed. (New York: Simon & Schuster, 1984), p. 24.

20. Thomas Paine, "Extract from a Reply to the Bishop of Llandaff," Stein 2, pp. 157–58.

21. See question #6 regarding the argument from design and the cosmological argument.

22. Or as the ancient Greek philosopher Thales is supposed to have said, "Everything is full of gods."

23. Anatole France, *Peter's Quotations: Ideas for Our Time* (New York: Bantam Books, 1977), p. 356.

Question #8

What's Wrong with Believing on Faith?

The question of faith often plays a major role in the belief system of many theists. Many Christians agree that there are no compelling arguments for the existence of god. They hold that belief in god is a matter of faith. Below is an examination of the possibility of believing on faith and some conclusive objections to it. Pascal's wager is an approach to belief in god which is related to faith. The wager is another popular method of attempting to justify belief in god. It will be shown that belief on the basis of faith, and on the basis of the wager, is insufficient to justify belief in god.

A. Faith is not an adequate justification for belief in god.

Because faith is often used as a justification for belief in god, it is important to explain why it fails as an adequate means of support for one's beliefs.

1. Faith is the firm belief in something for which there is no evidence.

Sometimes after explaining at length to someone that there are no good reasons for belief in god, that person may reply that his or her belief is a matter of faith. In *The Perfect Mirror? The Question of Bible Perfection,* Darrel Henschell mentions a sign he saw on a church in Springdale, Arkansas, which read: "Truth isn't a problem when faith isn't."[1] Many Christians treat the notion of faith as if faith itself were a sufficient reason to believe.

Faith is belief in the truth of something despite the fact that there is no evidence for that belief—or even when there is evidence to the contrary. Regarding faith, Bertrand Russell said:

> Christians hold that their faith does good, but other faiths do harm. . . . What I wish to maintain is that *all* faiths do harm. We may define "faith" as a firm belief in something for which there is no evidence. When there is evidence, no one speaks of "faith." We do not speak of faith that two and two are four or that the earth is round. We only speak of faith when we wish to substitute emotion for evidence.[2]

Romans 8:24–25 (*"Now hope that is seen is not hope. For who hopes for what he sees?"*) and Hebrews 11:1 (*"Now faith is the assurance of things hoped for, the conviction of things not seen"*) seem to support the definition of faith as belief in something for which there is no evidence.

Of course, since there are no good reasons (by that I mean no evidence) to believe in the existence of gods, and religious leaders have long been aware of this, it is no wonder that most of the religious systems of the world claim that believing for no reason is considered one of the greatest virtues. Why ask people to believe in something for *no* reason if there *are* reasons? It seems that the more faith one has—and thus the less reason needed for believing—the more revered that person is among believers. Pastors, priests, and other clergy will spend hours speaking to their flocks about the virtues of believing for no reason and how wonderful it all is, and what wonderful rewards await those who care the least about having reasons for their beliefs. As the risen Christ said to Thomas, "Blessed are they that have not seen and yet have believed" (John 20:29). Sometimes the clergy will try to make it out that faith is trust, commitment, or some other thing, but make no mistake about the nature of what they are promoting. Their explanations are just elaborate ways of telling believers to trust for no reason or to commit for no reason. They are asking people to abandon the need for evidence, for supporting reasons, for their beliefs.

Faith is the strong belief in the truth of a proposition in the absence of supporting evidence in its favor. Faith is believing for no reason.

So, what is wrong with all this? What's wrong with believing on the basis of faith?

2. There are conclusive objections to the "argument" from faith.

There are good reasons to believe that belief on the basis of faith is not only inadvisable from a pragmatic point of view but also immoral.

a. Faith is not a reason. It is an agreement that one has no reason.

Since faith is belief in the absence of supporting reasons, faith cannot be used *as a reason for belief.* After being shown that there are no good reasons to believe in gods, the religious person who says, "Ah, but you forget, that's where faith comes in!" is saying nothing other than "Ah, but you forget, that's where having no reasons comes in!" One who says, "No matter what you say, I still have my faith!" is merely saying "No matter what you say, I still have no reasons!"

To which the atheist may simply reply: "Correct!"

The strangest thing about the appeal to faith is that it really does not disagree with most of what the atheist asserts. The atheist is maintaining that the believer has no good reason to believe that there are gods. If the believer then states that it is a matter of faith, this is simply stating that the atheist's critique is correct—there are no good reasons.

Now the theist should not be tempted to reply, "I will accept that there are no reasons for belief in god, but I will then have faith that I am right anyway." That is simply saying that he or she has no reasons for his or her beliefs and no reasons to believe that he or she is right anyway. If having no reasons didn't work the first time, it won't work the second time. Faith in faith is pointless.

210

So the "argument" from faith is worthless as a support for belief. It is the acknowledgment that there *is* no support. As Friedrich Nietzsche said: "A casual stroll through the lunatic asylum shows that faith does not prove anything." Someone may believe something strongly, but that does not mean that his or her belief is true.

b. If one believes on faith, then one is more likely to adopt a false belief than a true one.

One who is concerned with holding true beliefs and avoiding false ones would be unwise to adopt a belief on the basis of faith.

(i) The New York City example shows the problems with faith.

Imagine that someone asks you to guess what sort of object, person, building, trash can, stray cat, or whatever is at the exact center of New York City at this moment. You are not allowed to make any investigation; you are not allowed to make any telephone calls, use a telescope, radar, or anything else. You just take a guess. What are the odds that you would be correct? Fifty-fifty? No. There are thousands of different things that could be at the center of New York City at that moment. Or, there may be nothing but grass or pavement.

Now suppose, without knowing the answer to the first question, that the person then asks you to guess the name of the person in the middle of New York City, if it does turn out that there is a person there. What do you think the odds are of both knowing that there is a person there *and* (if there is) of getting the name right? Not very good, obviously.

Suppose, further, that *if* there is a person, *and* you get the name right, that you are asked to guess what that person is thinking at that moment. Again, you are not allowed to make any investigation. Would you think you had a good or a poor chance of getting all these answers right?

Suppose that, instead of betting money on your answers, the person offering the bet wants you to bet your life. If you get any of the three questions above wrong, you die. Would you bet your life on your answers? No? Why not? Maybe you realize that it is more likely that you will be wrong than right.

(ii) The main tenets of theism are unlikely to be guessed correctly.

If one is asked to believe without evidence, on faith, this is no different from simply taking wild guesses. The theists ask potential converts to believe something for no reason, but not just any single belief. The potential convert has to believe, *for no reason,* a set of specific beliefs which are much more improbable than the previous New York City example. (At least it is known that there is a New York City. But no one has ever been able to show that there is a heaven, where it is, who inhabits it, or what sort of place it may be.) Thus, the potential convert must guess correctly about all of the following:

- There is at least one god.
- There is at most one god. (Of course, many other religions guess otherwise on this.)
- Of all the tens of thousands of gods throughout the history of religion, the one whom the the person *guesses* as correct really is the right one.
- You know what that god is thinking (i.e., you know what god's will is). After all, the convert will be asked to obey god's will.

212

Now, what are the odds that a person can get all those answers right just by guessing? Is it more likely that a person will be wrong about one of those answers or that he or she will be right? Clearly, it is more likely that someone will be wrong.

c. Believing on faith is a bad method of selecting beliefs.

The thousands of other religions in the world also ignore evidence, also believe on faith, and also simply guess about the existence and nature of gods. The typical Christian believes that all the other religions are incorrect. Thus, the Christian must acknowledge that most of the time, when someone believes on faith, that person reaches incorrect conclusions.

Further, there is no evidence that anyone who ever believes on faith is right. Thus, there is no evidence that Christianity is correct. Someone who believes something in the absence of evidence *ipso facto* admits that there is no evidence. Thus, the Christian who believes on faith admits that he or she is using a method of acquiring beliefs which is *known* to produce incorrect conclusions and is *never* known to produce true ones. Millions are known to be wrong when selecting beliefs in this way (according to the Christian), and no one is known to be correct. Is there a better definition of a bad method?

d. There are good reasons to believe that it is immoral to believe for no reason.

William K. Clifford (1845–1879), in an 1877 article titled "The Ethics of Belief," suggests that believing for no reason is not just imprudent, but immoral. Clifford argues that "It is wrong always, everywhere, and for anyone, to believe anything upon insufficient evidence."[3]

213

(i) Believing on faith makes one more likely to harm others.

Clifford gives the example of a ship owner with a number of pilgrims who have booked passage on his ship. The ship is in bad repair and very old, and to fix it would cost the ship owner some money out of his profit. So the ship owner, *for no reason,* decides to believe that the ship is seaworthy. He convinces himself that the people are not in danger and that they will be all right. He ignores the evidence before him and has faith. And, Clifford writes, after the ship sailed, the ship owner "got his insurance money when she went down in mid-ocean and told no tales."[4]

Now, wouldn't we say that the ship owner was *immoral* for ignoring the evidence? And even if the ship had arrived safely, wouldn't the ship owner still be just as immoral? Because he had no epistemic justification, no supporting reasons, to bring himself to believe that the ship was seaworthy, he had no *moral* justification to believe that either. One of Clifford's main points is that we have a duty not to harm others. He seems to be arguing along the following lines:

1. The more beliefs we have upon insufficient evidence, the more likely we are to have false beliefs. (Remember the New York City example.)
2. The more false beliefs we have, the more likely it is that we may harm others, whether intentionally or unintentionally (like the ship owner).
3. By (1)–(2), the more beliefs we have upon insufficient evidence, the more likely it is that we may harm others.
4. It is immoral to intentionally make oneself likely to harm others.

5. Therefore, it is immoral to intentionally adopt beliefs on insufficient evidence.

Clifford raises an important point regarding one's intentions. Even if one does not want to harm intentionally, one is more likely to harm another person if one has false beliefs than if one has true beliefs. Religious fundamentalists such as the Jehovah's Witnesses, who do not allow blood transfusions and other types of medical aid, are good examples here. Many of them have prayed for the health of their children instead of allowing physicians to assist, and they have, as a result, witnessed the deaths of their children because of their false beliefs.

(ii) Believing on faith becomes a bad habit.

Clifford also argues that once one accepts some beliefs without sufficient evidence, one may accept more and more such beliefs and end up a gullible fool. A person's belief in something, if accepted on faith, may lead him or her to accept other related beliefs. Suppose that a person, Ms. Canard, has the belief—on faith—that we all have angels who protect us. She then learns that someone has been killed in an automobile accident. Ms. Canard is forced to abandon the belief in guardian angels or accept some explanation, also without evidence. She may decide that one must pray in order to get the attention of a guardian angel and receive protection. She then asserts that the person killed did not pray. But then, suppose that another person who often prayed gets killed. Ms. Canard will have to accept another belief on faith. She may say that there is a special thing to do, such as communion, which is needed to make prayer effective. But then another person who prays and goes to communion gets killed. More and more unsupported beliefs must be adopted to save the first, and before long Ms. Canard has adopted a whole host of such beliefs. Once one has accepted some beliefs for no reason, there is little incentive not to continue to do so, and thus one increases the risk of harming

215

others or oneself because one ends up with a wide variety of beliefs which, as we saw earlier, are likely to be false.

d. It is in one's best interests not to be considered credulous.

Clifford also argues that it is in our best self-interests to not be credulous.

(A) If we are credulous, gullible, then people are less likely to believe what we say. One who believes on faith, after all, believes things without regard to evidence. One who believes on faith believes whatever sounds nice or pleases, not whatever is likely to be true. Because this method of selecting beliefs is clearly more likely to lead to error than truth, those who know that a person selects beliefs without evidence will be less likely to believe that person.

(B) If a person is known to be credulous, then others are more likely to lie to and take advantage of that person. The history of religion is a history rife with charlatans, fraud, forgery, and all manner of deception. Even today, those who argue in support of religion often resort to outright lies. They feel safe in the knowledge that their flock has been conditioned to accept mere assertions, to believe something simply because someone has said it. One who does not want to be hoodwinked by a mountebank should ask for evidence for claims and not simply believe assertions for no reason.

There are thus both moral and prudential reasons to refrain from believing on faith.

Summary of section A

These reasons seem conclusive against believing for no reason:

1. Faith is not a reason. It is an agreement that one has no reason.
2. If one believes on faith, then one is more likely to adopt a false belief than a true one.
3. There are good reasons to believe that it is immoral to believe on faith.
   a. Believing on faith makes one more likely to harm others.
   b. Believing on faith becomes a bad habit.
4. It is in one's best interests not to be considered credulous.
   a. People are less likely to believe someone who is gullible than someone who is not.
   b. People are more likely to take advantage of someone who is credulous than of someone who is not.

---

5. Therefore, believing on faith is a poor method of selecting beliefs.
6. A poor method of selecting beliefs is an insufficient justification for a given belief.

Therefore, believing on faith is an insufficient justification for belief in god.

It is unfortunate that one need give any arguments as to why one should refrain from believing without evidence, but the well-polished religious machinery that is still operative in our culture makes belief for no reason seem so innocuous, so noble, that it is often easy to forget that one ought to ask for evidence for one's beliefs.

It is interesting to note that many Christians who admit that they have no evidence for their belief, who assert that belief in the absence of evidence is justified, will react strangely when told, "There is no god." The first thing they do in response to this assertion is to ask for evidence!

B. Pascal's wager fails as a justification for belief in god.

French mathematician, physicist, and inventor Blaise Pascal (1623–1662) is well known in the area of religion for his presentation of an argument which has come to be known as "Pascal's wager."

1. Pascal's wager addresses the possible benefits and costs of belief.

On November 23, 1654, Pascal experienced his "night of fire," an intense mystical experience which made him extremely pious. He joined the Jansenists, a heretical sect of the Roman Catholic Church. Pascal wanted to find some way to convert his friends, most of whom were ex-Catholics. Thus, he devised an argument, published in his *Pensées* in 1670, which is often used in a modified form today. Although Pascal did not make use of the concept of punishment for nonbelief, most popular forms of his wager include this element.

Briefly, here is a one common form of the wager, similar to Pascal's:

1. Everyone is either a believer or a nonbeliever. The category of "nonbeliever" encompasses both agnostics (those who suspend judgment about god's existence) and atheists (who deny that there are gods).
2. Both the believer and the nonbeliever will be either correct or incorrect about the existence of god.
3. If you are a believer, and you are *correct* that god exists, then after your death you will gain eternal reward.
4. If you are not a believer and you are *correct* that god does not exist, you will live and die and you will not get any reward after your death.
5. If the believer is *incorrect*, there is no loss. Since it costs you nothing to believe in god, then if you believe and you are wrong, you lose nothing.
6. If the nonbeliever is *incorrect*, he or she will be tortured for eternity.

Thus, if you are a believer, you have a chance to gain eternal reward, but if you are not a believer, you have no chance for it. Win or lose, the believer comes out ahead of the nonbeliever. Therefore, suggests Pascal, it is in your best interests to take the chance, accept the wager, and believe in god. The believer has nothing to lose and everything to gain, whereas the nonbeliever can gain nothing and risks losing everything.

2. *There are conclusive objections to Pascal's wager.*

The wager fails. Despite its popularity and appeal, it is subject to devastating objections, only some of which are outlined below.

a. *It is false that it costs nothing to accept the wager.*

Those who propose the wager try to suggest that it costs one nothing to believe in god, but there is a high cost. One sacrifices an interest in believing what is true and in rejecting what is false.

(i) The wager makes truth irrelevant to one's method of choosing beliefs.

One who proposes the wager is suggesting that we should hold beliefs based on what rewards they promise, not based on whether they are true. If the theist is not at all concerned with truth, then he or she can accept the wager. Yet surely one who decides that truth is irrelevant to belief sacrifices integrity. How much is your intellectual integrity worth? How much is believing the truth worth to you? Should we intentionally allow ourselves to adopt beliefs regardless of their truth simply because they sound pleasant?

(ii) All the objections against belief on faith apply to belief based on the wager.

Belief based on the wager, like belief on faith, is not concerned with truth, so all of the objections to belief on the basis of faith apply to the wager.

(A) If you are basing belief merely on the possibility of reward,

220

and not on likelihood of truth, then you are *far* more likely to be wrong than if you only believe what is likely to be true instead of whatever system of belief makes the grandest promises.

(B) As Clifford's arguments have shown with regard to believing on faith, it is immoral to believe because of the wager. One is likely to acquire a false belief if one operates according to the wager, and thus one would be more likely to harm others. The same argument applies here.

(C) It is in one's best interests not to be considered credulous. One who believes certain propositions because of promises, and not because one has considered the truth of those propositions, could be considered credulous.

Therefore, as in the case of believing on faith, belief based on the wager is insufficient justification for belief in god.

b. It is clearly false that it is a good idea to believe something solely because of a potential reward.

Is it a good idea to do something because of a potential reward without regard to whether it is true? It seems that it is not.

Perhaps an example will help. Suppose that you receive in the mail an offer for the best car ever made. All you have to do is send *all* your money to an address in Beeville, Texas, and within six months you will have, delivered to your door, a car so amazing, so wonderful, that you cannot even imagine it. No photo of the car or any other details are enclosed. The ad says that no photo could do it justice.

Now, after checking with the local authorities, you discover that no one has ever been known to accept this offer, send in their money, and get the car, but *millions* of people have been known to send in their money and get absolutely nothing. Would you send all your money? Why wouldn't you? If truth is not a criterion for adopting beliefs, if all that matters is to take a chance because there may be a wonderful reward, then the wager indicates that you should take the chance.

Note that in the car example millions have been known to send in their money and get nothing in return. These millions are analogous to the millions of people in other religions who have accepted the wager with respect to their gods, and who, according to the Christian, will never receive the reward they were promised.

So here we have a situation where millions have been *known* to be wrong when they followed this line of reasoning, the wager, and *none* have been known to get the reward. This sounds like another description of an unreliable method of selecting beliefs.

c. It cannot be shown that there is only one religion which may be true.

For the wager to work, even if there were no other objections, one would have to assume that only one religion has a chance of being true. Because this cannot be shown, the wager fails.

(i) The many-gods objection shows that the wager fails.

If it cannot be shown that there is only one religion which may be true, then one who wishes to accept the wager will be unable to decide which religion to accept. Among theists there are many who say that their way is the *only* way to get saved. Other religions have their route to salvation. Or nirvana. Are the Hindus correct? Were the ancient Greeks? Even among Christians there is no agreement about which denomination is the correct one. Many fundamentalist Christians hold that Roman Catholics will go straight to hell. John Calvin had the Spanish doctor Servetus slow-roasted alive for denying the doctrine of the trinity. Which religion is the one to wager on, and which denomination? Even if Pascal's wager were to work, it would merely suggest that one is supposed to take a chance on religion and try to gain a reward, but there is no nonarbitrary way to decide which religion is the one to accept. If truth and evidence are irrelevant to the adoption of a belief, then there is no way to tell which religion should be adopted. They are not all the same, and, as they themselves insist, not all of them are true. The wager is in serious trouble if there are many religions and denominations available, and, of course, there are.

(ii) The damnation objection makes the wager unappealing.

If there are at least two religions which have some chance of being true, and each promises damnation for those who believe the wrong religion, then it would be dangerous to believe in the wrong one. The attractiveness of the wager breaks down completely here.

If belief in one religion, which turns out to be incorrect, means that one will be damned by the god of a competing religion, then the risk of loss and the promise of gain in two different religions cancel each other out. The supposed reward of one is canceled out by the risk of damnation in the other. By the same token, the risk of damnation in one religion is canceled out by the promise of reward in its competitor, so the motive for taking a chance, for wagering, is eliminated. In a gain-loss analysis the whole thing is a wash. The potential gains are canceled out by the potential losses and the expected value of the wager, as the probability theorists call it, is zero. There is no advantage to the wager if there are at least two competing religions which promise damnation to those who believe another religion, and there are such competing religions.

d. The wager will not recommend Christianity.

Most theists who propose the wager use it to support Christianity. However, if some religion other than Christianity promises a better heaven or a worse hell, Pascal's wager will work against Christianity.

There are biblical verses which suggest that there are levels of heaven (2 Cor. 12:2, for example). Suppose that some other religion promises to all of its followers only the best possible heaven, and threatens all disbelievers with only the worst possible hell. Suppose also that this same religion has a much lower threshold for entrance to heaven than does any other religion. In this case, then, the wager would *clearly* result in the conclusion that one should abandon Christianity and adopt this other religion.

There are many religions in the world, some of which make grander promises and greater threats than Christianity. It is unlikely that the wager would recommend Christianity. At the very least, Christians should not assume blindly that the wager would support Christianity.

Summary of section B

a. It is false that it costs nothing to accept the wager.
b. It is clearly false that it is a good idea to believe something solely because of a potential reward.
c. It cannot be shown that there is only *one* religion which may be true.
d. The wager will not recommend Christianity.

Therefore, Pascal's wager is insufficient justification for belief in god.

Conclusion

It has been suggested that it is both immoral and imprudent to believe on faith. These and other objections also apply to Pascal's wager. Both faith and the wager fail as supports for belief in god.

A rational person often has a hard time understanding how anyone would think that it is a good thing to believe for no reason, but there are many things about theism which are difficult to fathom. Of course, the main reason that people believe in god has nothing to do with the truth of this belief. Most people believe in god because that is what they were taught to do when they were young. As they mature, and no reasons can be found for this belief, many people eventually accept the opinion of the clergy that supporting reasons are superfluous. This is unfortunate. As Bertrand Russell noted:

> There is something feeble, and a little contemptible, about a man who cannot face the perils of life without the help of comfortable myths. Almost inevitably some part of him is aware that they are myths and that he believes them only because they are comforting. But he dare not face this thought, and he therefore cannot carry his own reflections to any logical conclusion. Moreover, since he is aware, however dimly, that his opinions are not rational, he becomes furious when they are disputed.[5]

Someone who appeals to belief without evidence recognizes that the belief is indefensible. It is to be hoped that those who hear the request for belief in the absence of reasons will respect themselves too much to allow themselves to fall for a lot of empty promises simply because they are promises. One's life is too important a commodity to give away to just any set of beliefs.

Notes

1. Henschell, *The Perfect Mirror? The Question of Bible Perfection* (Fayetteville, Ariz.: Hairy Tickle Press, 1996), p. 88.

2. Bertrand Russell, "Are the World's Troubles Due to Decay of Faith?" reprinted in *Bertrand Russell on God and Religion*, Al Seckel, ed. (Amherst, N.Y.: Prometheus Books, 1986), p. 283.

3. William Clifford, "The Ethics of Belief," reprinted in Stein, p. 282.

4. Ibid., p. 277.

5. Bertrand Russell, "Are the World's Troubles Due to Decay of Faith?" reprinted in *Bertrand Russell on God and Religion*, p. 286.

Conclusion

There is much more to say about atheism. Since so little is known about this view, it is to be expected that there will remain a number of unanswered questions, both those regarding issues unaddressed here and those regarding details which I did not have space to explain. Included is a list of resource material, where further questions may be answered.

One of the important things to remember when investigating atheism is to keep separate which questions are about atheism and which are about something else. For example, people often ask me questions about such matters as love, coping with death, specific ethical issues, and so on, expecting to receive an answer which represents "*the* atheist's view." There is no such view. There is Doug Krueger's view, Kurt Vonnegut's, Bertrand Russell's, Carl Sagan's, George Carlin's, Randy Newman's, and many others. We may share a number of beliefs, but, if we do, it is not because that is *the* atheist's view. It may be, instead, that we share certain principles about the love of truth, the investigation of the world, or

227

because we consider life too valuable to devote to the first nice-sounding *Weltanschauung* to come along. I do know that we have rejected theism, and that we have that in common, at least.

To be sure, I and many other atheists have well-developed philosophical positions on many subjects, from love and death to art and politics, and on a number of other important issues. These views are the result of careful and conscientious investigations into these matters, investigations freed from the constraints of dogma and superstition, which are allowed to follow truth wherever it may lead and not just within the boundaries allotted by centuries-old systems of ignorance and bigotry. The rejection of theism opens up new and exciting avenues of thought. One's beliefs regarding everything from the foundations of ethics to the empirical investigation of the world may be examined afresh with a clear conscience, and with an eye toward understanding instead of blind acceptance.

To some, this prospect may seem frightening. Thinking for oneself, not passively accepting dogma, is the hallmark of a freethinker, and it is the first step on the road to atheism and the road to truth. A comment from Bertrand Russell's "The Value of Free Thought" is appropriate here:

> The free thinker's universe may seem bleak and cold to those who have been accustomed to the comfortable indoor warmth of the Christian cosmology. But to those who have grown accustomed to it, it has its own sublimity, and confers its own joys. In learning to think freely we have learnt to thrust fear out of our thoughts, and this lesson, once learnt, brings a kind of peace which is impossible to the slave of hesitant and uncertain credulity.[1]

The freethinker may examine the vast array of human ideas, past and present, and consider options hitherto unimagined. At any stage in the inquiry, when confronted with the claim that such-and-such is the case, he or she may *ask for justification of the claim.* Furthermore, the freethinker may *expect an answer, not a mystery, not absurdity, not an insult to one's intelligence.*

The freethinker need not be satisfied any longer with nonsensical explanations such as: beings who make things happen by magic powers; omnipotent and transcendent beings who can do anything logically possible except perform any action whatsoever; infinitely merciful beings who callously slaughter millions; gods who pretend to make a sacrifice by dying but who are really immortal; gods of love who condemn everyone to eternal torture for the disobedience of a distant ancestor; gods who are appeased only by a human sacrifice (such as Jesus); a just god who believes that the guilty may go scot-free as long as an innocent man (such as Jesus) suffers an agonizing death in their place—or, if Jesus is thought to be god: a god who sees everyone sinning and decides to drown everyone, and then sees everyone sinning thousands of years later and decides that the solution is to kill himself to keep people from being sent to eternal torture; omnibenevolent gods who can stop the sun in its daily course but who refuse to lend a hand to the tens of thousands of children who die annually of starvation worldwide, and so on. These absurdities, and scores of others like them, which churches routinely require the pious to adopt, confuse human thought and, like a computer virus, impede the clear mental operations of the thinking mind.[2]

I hope that if you are a theist now you will take the information in this book seriously and embark on that wonderful adventure which is the love of truth by investigating the truth of theistic claims. Atheism can be an important element in a worldview, and it should be part of yours. But it should not be adopted simply because of its pragmatic advantages. It should be adopted because it is true.

There are no gods.

Summary of the argument
Against Belief in Gods:

1. The assertion that a god exists is an extraordinary claim.
2. If there is no credible evidence for an extraordinary claim, then one should conclude that the extraordinary claim is false.
3. There is no credible evidence for the existence of any gods.
    i. The bible is unreliable; it cannot be considered credible evidence.
    ii. Reports of miracles cannot be considered credible evidence.
    iii. Philosophical arguments for the existence of gods fail and cannot be considered credible evidence.
    iv. Faith is an insufficient justification for belief in gods.
    v. Pascal's wager is an insufficient justification for belief in gods.
4. There is good evidence that the traditional god does not exist.
    i. The concept of god is self-contradictory; such a being *cannot* exist.
    ii. The existence of evil is evidence against the existence of the traditional god.
    iii. The existence of nonbelievers is evidence against the existence the traditional god.

Therefore, one should conclude that there are no gods.

Notes

1. Bertrand Russell, "The Value of Free Thought," reprinted in *Bertrand Russell on God and Religion*, Al Seckel, ed. (Amherst, N.Y.: Prometheus Books, 1986), p. 269.

2. Some people complain that I reduce Christianity to absurdity. I usually reply that it has already been reduced about as much as it can be simply in its exposition.

Suggested Readings

This annotated list of suggested readings is included to encourage and assist the reader in pursuing further questions.

Barker, Dan. *Losing Faith in Faith: From Preacher to Atheist.* Madison, Wis.: The Freedom From Religion Foundation, Inc., 1992. A very readable account of the events which led a committed Christian to reject his religion and his ministry. Chapters include discussions of the historical evidence for Jesus, bible contradictions, biblical morality, and related issues. The author is now on the staff of the Freedom from Religion Foundation, Inc.

Basil, R., M. B. Gehrman, and T. Madigan, eds. *On the Barricades: Religion and Free Inquiry in Conflict.* Amherst, N.Y.: Prometheus Books, 1989. An excellent anthology, with articles on subjects such as humanism, biblical criticism, faith healing, ethics, and more.

Callahan, Tim. *Bible Prophecy: Failure or Fulfillment?* Altadena, Calif.: Millennium Press, 1997. An examination of claims of biblical prophecy from the Old Testament to the Book of Revelation. Included is a section on contemporary attempts to interpret prophecy in light of apocalyptic expectations.

Drange, Theodore M. *Nonbelief and Evil: Two Arguments for the Nonexistence of God.* Amherst, N.Y.: Prometheus Books, 1998. A detailed analysis of these two strong arguments for atheism. Drange is extremely thorough, and he anticipates, and rebuts, many variations on standard objections.

Helms, Randel. *Gospel Fictions.* Amherst, N.Y.: Prometheus Books, 1988. Helms explains how an examination of literary relationships between various bible stories reveals how many of them, rather than being historical, are merely rewrites of other stories. There are chapters on nativity legends, miracles, the passion narratives, and resurrection legends.

Henschell, Darrel. *The Perfect Mirror? The Question of Bible Perfection.* Fayetteville, Ariz.: HairyTickle Press, 1996. This short, well-done introduction to the hundreds of biblical errors and contradictions is available for $14.00 post paid from: HairyTickle Press, 2367–1 Green Acres Rd., Suite 127, Fayetteville, AZ 72703. There are chapters on Christian doctrine, the Old and New Testaments, prophecy, the doctrine of biblical inerrancy, and more. Highly recommended for those who think that the bible is free of error.

Hume, David. *Dialogues Concerning Natural Religion.* Norman Kemp Smith, ed. New York: Macmillan Publishing Co., 1947. Hume's *Dialogues,* published posthumously in 1779, presents a more detailed critique of the argument from design than what is found in the *Enquiry Concerning Human Understanding* (see below), and it has become a classic.

———. *An Enquiry Concerning Human Understanding.* Eric Steinberg, ed. Indianapolis, Ind.: Hackett Publishing Co., 1993. The *Enquiry* was first published in 1748, but section X, "Of Miracles," is still one of the best critiques of the problem of accepting testimony about miracles. Section XI, "Of a Particular Providence and of a Future State," regarding the argument from design, is a short, well-argued attack of that position.

234

Kurtz, Paul. *Exuberance: A Philosophy of Happiness.* Amherst, N.Y.: Prometheus Books, 1977. In this nontechnical work, a philosopher explains how to maintain a healthy zest for life, how to have a positive approach to facing death, the importance of love and friendship, and other related subjects, all without belief in god.

————. *Forbidden Fruit: The Ethics of Humanism.* Amherst, N.Y.: Prometheus Books, 1988. Kurtz explains his system of ethics, which does not require gods. Common moral decencies, ethical education for children, human rights, the meaning of life, and more are covered in this nontechnical, highly recommended book.

Lamont, Corliss. *The Philosophy of Humanism.* New York: Continuum Publishing Company, 1990. This philosopher, social activist, and honorary president of the American Humanist Association explains in nontechnical terms the history and influence of humanism, a humanist theory of the nature of the universe, the role of reason and science in the humanist view, the ethics of humanism, and other topics.

Le Poidevin, Robin. *Defending Atheism: An Introduction to the Philosophy of Religion.* New York: Routledge, 1996. An excellent introductory work, well suited to beginning philosophy students, or anyone without a background in philosophy, to develop additional familiarity with the arguments before tackling more complex works.

Mack, Burton. *The Book of Q and Christian Origins.* New York, N.Y.: HarperCollins Publishers, 1995.

————. *Who Wrote the New Testament? The Making of the Christian Myth.* New York, N.Y.: HarperCollins Publishers, 1993. In these two books, a noted bible scholar explains in detail the origins of the New Testament and the Christian bible, and he shows how most Christians have a completely mistaken idea of how these books came to be written. The social and political environment which influenced the writings, as well as the specific goals of the authors, are examined.

Mackie, J. L. *The Miracle of Theism: Arguments for and against the Existence of God.* Oxford: Clarendon Press, 1982. An advanced introduction to atheism, intended for those with at least some familiarity with the philosophy of religion, but also accessible to general readers. Historical, as well as contemporary arguments by apologists, are analyzed.

Martin, Michael. *Atheism: A Philosophical Justification.* Philadelphia, Pa.: Temple University Books, 1990. A skilled philosopher carefully examines the best arguments for the existence of god, both historical and contemporary, and he shows how, one and all, they fail. Detailed, technical, but effective and thorough.

————. *The Big Domino in the Sky and Other Atheistic Tales.* Amherst, N.Y.: Prometheus Books, 1997. An anthology of short stories, from science fiction to historical, which illustrate some important philosophical point about theism and atheism. Well crafted and very readable.

————. *The Case against Christianity.* Philadelphia, Pa.: Temple University Books, 1991. In this book, not as technical as his previous work, Martin carefully examines arguments against Christianity, the best defenses that contemporary apologists can invent, and objections that show that the defenses fail. Highly recommended.

McKinsey, C. Dennis. *The Encyclopedia of Biblical Errancy.* Amherst, N.Y.: Prometheus Books, 1995. A huge, well documented, carefully researched gold mine of biblical errors, contradictions, and fallacies. Voltaire said of the gospels that there are almost as many errors as words. McKinsey shows that this applies to other parts of the bible as well.

Metzger, Bruce M., and Michael D. Coogan, eds. *The Oxford Companion to the Bible.* New York: Oxford University Press, 1993. An excellent resource for those who want the facts, not the fiction, about the books of the bible. Written from a scholarly, impartial, not necessarily skeptical point of view.

Nickell, Joe. *Looking for a Miracle.* Amherst, N.Y.: Prometheus Books, 1993. An investigator surveys many reports of paranormal, supernatural, and miraculous occurrences, and presents naturalistic, scientific explanations for these mysteries. There are discussions of the shroud of Turin, the image of Guadalupe, weeping statues, speaking in tongues, snake handling, faith healing, visions, stigmata, and much more.

Nielsen, Kai. *Ethics without God.* Amherst, N.Y.: Prometheus Books, 1990. An anthology of powerful essays which defend humanistic ethics, critique theistic morality, explain the role of human existence and death in relation to morality, and other important topics.

Pojman, Louis. *Ethics: Discovering Right and Wrong.* Belmont, Calif.: Wadsworth Publishing Co., 1995. A good, short introduction to a number of ethical theories, most of which do not require god. This book is often used in college-level introductory courses in ethics.

Randi, James. *The Faith Healers.* Amherst, N.Y.: Prometheus Books, 1987. A revealing and witty investigation into the careers of contemporary faith healers, from Oral Roberts to Peter Popoff and others.

Smith, George H. *Atheism: The Case against God.* Amherst, N.Y.: Prometheus Books, 1989. A thorough, but nontechnical, explanation of atheism, and a critique of various aspects of Christianity.

Smith, Morton. *Jesus the Magician.* New York: Barnes & Noble Books, 1978. An investigation into the gospel accounts of Jesus which shows that the reports of his miracles fit a common pattern of magic spells and healing rituals performed by many other "miracle" workers of that time.

Stiebing, William H. *Out of the Desert? Archaeology and the Exodus/Conquest Narratives.* Amherst, N.Y.: Prometheus Books, 1989. A scholarly summary of archaeological findings which shows that the biblical accounts of the exodus and later wars of conquest are not supported by the facts.

Stein, Gordon, ed. *An Anthology of Atheism and Rationalism.* Amherst, N.Y.: Prometheus Books, 1980.

———. *A Second Anthology of Atheism and Rationalism.* Amherst, N.Y.: Prometheus Books, 1987. These two anthologies contain excellent essays on atheism and agnosticism, many of which had been out of print for over half a century. Topics include the existence of god, the devil, morality, revealed religion, and others. The second anthology even contains some poetry.

Stenger, Victor J. *Not By Design.* Amherst, N.Y.: Prometheus Books, 1988. A physicist explains how order can and does emerge from chaos every day. This is an excellent, nontechnical presentation of the findings of contemporary physics, and Stenger shows how these findings destroy the theological argument from design.

Wells, G. A. *Did Jesus Exist?* London: Pemberton, 1986. Also distributed through Prometheus Books, Amherst, N.Y. Wells examines all the historical evidence for the existence of Jesus, from early Christian writings and letters to later Jewish and pagan testimonies, and he presents a solid case for the view that Jesus never existed.

———. *The Jesus Legend.* Chicago: Open Court, 1996. A carefully researched, well-developed account of how the Jesus legend could have arisen even in the absence of any such historical figure. Christians sometimes argue that Jesus must have existed because reports of his supposed exploits spread so quickly after his reported demise that they must be based on actual events. This book solidly refutes that view.

Organizations and Internet Sites

An atheist in a world of theists can feel terribly out of place. Fortunately, there are organizations that can provide information and support on many levels. Most of these organizations have Internet addresses. The Internet allows people to access easily information about atheism, biblical criticism, humanism, claims of miracles, and other issues—information that was in many cases difficult or almost impossible to find before the information revolution. Below are the addresses of a few organizations and sites which can serve as valuable resources.

American Atheists: http://www.atheist.org

Founded in 1963, this high-profile, often controversial organization publishes books, pamphlets, cards, the magazine *American Atheist*, and other material. Catalog and membership inquiries can be sent to: American Atheists, P.O. Box 2117, Austin, TX 78768–2117.

The American Humanist Association

This organization publishes books, distributes audio and video tapes, organizes conferences, and gets socially and politically involved in the realization of humanist goals of life. They publish the magazine *The Humanist*. Address subscription inquiries to: The American Humanist Association, 7 Harwood Drive, P.O. Box 1188, Amherst, NY 14226–7188.

The Committee for the Scientific Investigation of Claims of the Paranormal (CSICOP): http://www.csicop.org

As their name suggests, this open-minded group examines purported data for paranormal activity of all sorts, including dowsing, ESP, faith healing, out-of-body experiences, astrology, UFOs, and other such claims. Inquiries about their monthly magazine, *The Skeptical Inquirer*, may be sent to: Skeptical Inquirer, Box 703, Amherst, NY 14226-0703.

The Council for Secular Humanism:
http://www.secularhumanism.org

The philosophical, practical, and political sides of nonbelief are addressed by this organization, which also publishes the quarterly magazine *Free Inquiry*. The address for subscription information is: Free Inquiry, P.O. Box 664, Amherst, NY 14226-0664.

The Freedom from Religion Foundation, Inc:
http://www.infidels.org/org/ffrf/

This organization publishes *Freethought Today*, which they describe as "the only freethought newspaper in the United States." They also have books, music, T-shirts, and other material. It may be the only place that sells a "Nothing Fails Like Prayer" bumper sticker. Address inquiries to: The Freedom from Religion Foundation, Inc. (FFRF, Inc.), P.O. Box 750, Madison, WI 53701.

The Secular Web: http://www.infidels.org

Run by the Internet Infidels, this site has many documents, both modern and historical, on every issue from biblical criticism to critiques of arguments for the existence of god. In addition, one can join e-mail lists, obtain information about scheduled debates, find local freethought organizations, and more.

The Skeptical Review

A bimonthly newsletter edited by Farrell Till, which specializes in the exposition of biblical error, contradiction, and absurdity. Till also runs an e-mail list on the same subject. The newsletter provides a forum for inerrantists, with appropriate responses by Till and others. The first year's subscription is free. Back issues can be found online through the Secular Web. The newsletter address is: The Skeptical Review, P.O. Box 717, Canton, IL 61520-0717.

The Skeptics Society: http://www.skeptic.com/

The publishers of *Skeptic* magazine maintain this web site, which touches on such varied topics as New Age therapies, reports of paranormal phenomena, creationism, fringe social and political movements, questionable economic theories, and much more. The address for subscriptions to *Skeptic* is: Skeptic, P.O. Box 338, Altadena, CA 91001.